FAIR AMERICA

WORLD'S FAIRS IN THE UNITED STATES

Robert W. Rydell,
John E. Findling, and
Kimberly D. Pelle

SMITHSONIAN BOOKS
Washington and New York

TO OUR FAMILIES

Editor: Ruth G. Thomson
Designer: Janice Wheeler

Library of Congress Cataloging-in-Publication Data
Rydell, Robert W.
    Fair America : world's fairs in the United States / Robert W. Rydell,
John E. Findling, Kimberly D. Pelle
        p.   cm.
    Includes bibliographical references.
    ISBN 1-56098-968-8 (hardcover : alk. paper). — ISBN 1-56098-384-1
(pbk. : alk. paper)
    1. Trade shows—United States—History—19th century.   2. Trade shows—
United States—History—20th century.   I. Findling, John E. II. Pelle, Kimberly D.
III. Title.
T395.5.U6R934   2000
907.4′73—dc21   99-40957

British Library Cataloguing-in-Publication Data are available

Manufactured in the United States of America
16 15 14 13 12   7 6 5 4

For permission to reproduce illustrations appearing in this book, please correspond
directly with the owners of the works, as listed in the individual captions. The
Smithsonian Institution Press does not retain reproduction rights for these illustrations
individually or maintain a file of addresses for photo sources.

CONTENTS

LIST OF ILLUSTRATIONS

ACKNOWLEDGMENTS

*A*t the outset we need to make clear that this book would not have been possible without the work of many scholars who have helped make world's fairs an object of growing academic interest. We are also indebted to the many world's fair collectors, documentary filmmakers, and enthusiasts whose own publications, productions, and collections have paved the way for this book.

At the Smithsonian Institution Press Mark Hirsch has encouraged our efforts to produce a general history of America's world's fairs for an audience of specialists and nonspecialists alike. We also had the good fortune to secure the talents of Ruth Thomson, who has made it seem as if this book is the product of a single voice when, in fact, it is the product of three.

Over the years librarians and archivists around the United States have been gracious in helping us to make sense of the multiple and overlaid tracks left by world's fairs. We particularly wish to acknowledge the assistance received from the interlibrary loan departments at Montana State University and Indiana University Southeast. Librarians and archivists at the City Archives of Philadelphia, the University of Illinois at Chicago, and the Missouri Historical Society have also gone out of their ways to respond to our many queries. For many years the librarians and archivists at the following two institutions have borne the brunt of incessant requests for information about world's fairs. At the Smithsonian Institution Libraries we wish to thank particularly Nancy E. Gwinn for her decision to make the Smithsonian Institution Libraries' collection of published books and pamphlets available on microfilm. We are also grateful to the Smithsonian's archival and library staff, especially Bill Cox and Rhoda Ratner, for their support. Far from Washington, D.C., in the Sanoian Special Collections Library in the Henry Madden Library at California State University at Fresno, we are also grateful to Tammy Lau, Ronald Mahoney, and Jean Coffey for all of their assistance and expert advice over the years. This book would not exist were it not for them.

Other people have supported us in our work. Sheila Andersen, David Campbell, Jake Newman, Marja Rojoll, Sam Sloss, and Frank Thackeray all deserve special mention. We are also grateful to Professors Thomas J. Schlereth, Eric J. Sandeen, and Keith Walden, who reviewed this manuscript during various stages of its preparation.

Finally, three individuals have come to our aid more times than we can count. Under the heading of love and support, Kim Pelle wishes to thank her mother, Barbara Gasperetti; John Findling wishes to thank his wife, Carol; and Robert Rydell wishes to thank his wife, Kiki.

INTRODUCTION

*L*ong before the Internet and the World Wide Web, another network—a veritable web—of world's fairs ringed the globe, giving form and substance to the modern world. The world's fair movement originated in London, in 1851, with the Crystal Palace Exhibition. From there world's fairs became the rage in Europe and even excited the fantasies of several New Yorkers, including newspaper editor Horace Greeley and showman P. T. Barnum, who organized a crystal palace of their own in 1853 only to have it overwhelmed by the growing sectional crisis that, within a decade, would result in the American Civil War. Another twenty-three years would pass before world's fairs took root in American soil. But once they did, world's fairs, sometimes called international expositions or exhibitions, would spread across the American cultural landscape, defining its form and content and influencing the lives of tens of millions of fairgoers who made world's fairs a part of their lives.

To say that world's fairs have exerted a formative influence on the way Americans have thought about themselves and the world in which they live probably understates the importance of those expositions. World's fairs have been sources of much pleasure, inspiring the creation of Coney Island and other amusement parks and subsequent theme parks like Disneyland. Fairs have introduced generations of Americans to pathbreaking scientific and technological innovations like telephones, X rays, infant incubators, television, moving walkways, asphalt, and plastics. The architecture and parklike settings of world's fairs, along with their sometimes visionary schemes for public and private transportation, have influenced the ways our cities and small towns look and the way we behave in them. The importance of world's fairs is undeniable.

Or are we exaggerating? Were world's fairs held simply to amuse the masses? Are they best regarded as cultural ephemera, money-losing propositions, for the most part, that, for all of their visual excitement, have no long-term significance? Surely, world's fairs cannot be considered on the same order as wars, or revolutions, or famous presidential decisions—the stuff of traditional history. Perhaps world's fairs should be regarded as interesting sideshows on the margins of American society and culture, something to be relegated to the category of leisure.

Those objections to making world's fairs a central element of study within the broader subject of American—indeed, world—history are not unimportant. Those same objections have been raised about teaching popular culture more generally. If the study of popular, or mass, culture is trivial, then surely a book about world's fairs is a waste of time. Shouldn't students be reading about famous men and women who shaped the American political, diplomatic, and economic tradition?

Students certainly need to learn more about America's movers and shakers. And one good reason for studying world's fairs is precisely because they were initiated by those in positions of power and influence. To examine the roster of world's fair designers and managers is to examine a who's who of prominent Americans, ranging from businessmen like John Wanamaker and Henry Ford to presidents like William McKinley and Franklin Delano Roosevelt to political activists like Frederick Douglass and Ida B. Wells. The list includes scientists Joseph Henry and Karl Compton and social scientists Franz Boas and E. Franklin Frazier, not to mention inventors like Thomas Edison. Influential historians like Hubert Howe Bancroft wrote official histories of fairs, while others, like Charles Beard, edited a book series in conjunction with a world's fair. Another historian, Frederick Jackson Turner, presented his famous paper on the significance of the frontier in American history in conjunction with a fair, while yet another, Henry Adams, made world's fairs into one of the cornerstones of his famous autobiography.[1]

And what about artists, sculptors, musicians, architects, and engineers? For artists Mary Cassatt and Aaron Douglass; sculptors Daniel Chester

Early world's fairs attracted millions of people. Here the Joy Zone at the 1915 Panama-Pacific International Exposition is packed with crowds. (Photo courtesy of John E. Findling)

French, Karl Bitter, and Leo Friedlander; musicians John Philip Sousa and George Gershwin; urban planners Daniel Burnham and Robert Moses; architects Louis Skidmore, Nathaniel Owings, and Edward Durell Stone; and engineers George Ferris and Luther Stieringer, to name only a few, world's fairs provided unequaled opportunities for those men and women to leave their mark on American culture. The world of entertainment and world's fairs shared a close relationship as expositions featured stars and impresarios such as Buffalo Bill, Sol Bloom, Billy Rose, Sally Rand, and a host of Hollywood and Broadway stars. From the vantage point of most of the men and women who organized displays and shows, or performed in them, world's fairs seemed to be worthwhile endeavors. The same can be said for most of the millions of ordinary Americans from all walks of life who visited America's international expositions.

The study of world's fairs not only affords insights into America's cultural authorities but also opens windows on the lives and values of ordinary Americans who traveled to fairs in stunning numbers. Between the Philadelphia Centennial International Exhibition of 1876 and World War I, American world's fairs attracted about 100 million visitors. Between the

Picture postcards first became available for the Chicago World's Columbian Exposition in 1893. (Photo courtesy of John E. Findling)

world wars attendance at America's fairs ran about the same. Then, in the postwar era, attendance at the 1964–65 New York World's Fair alone topped fifty-one million, while attendance at smaller fairs in Seattle (1962), San Antonio (1968), Spokane (1974), Knoxville (1982), and New Orleans (1984) totaled around thirty million.

Of course, one did not have to travel to fairs to be affected by their lure. Even before movie theaters featured world's fair newsreels and feature films, world's fair promoters were positively ingenious in their public relations stunts. Sponsors of America's fairs in the nineteenth and early twentieth centuries, for instance, involved a vast number of children in organizing state and local exhibits for expositions that they might never see in person. Those children, like millions of adults, would also encounter fairs secondhand through press accounts and picture postcards—an innovation in mass communication inspired by world's fairs.

In recent years popular interest in world's fairs has slipped somewhat because fairs now compete with a variety of electronic media and theme parks that, ironically, world's fairs helped to nurture in the first place. Even so, Miami and Los Angeles, among other cities, have discussed bids to host world's fairs in upcoming years. In addition world's fairs continue to thrive in Europe as evidenced by expositions in Seville (1992), Lisbon (1998), and Hannover (2000). To reveal our conclusion at the outset: it would take a rash prophet indeed to forecast the end of world's fairs in the postmodern world. As we enter the twenty-first century, we believe that world's fairs will continue to be a powerful medium for addressing, and perhaps deflecting, deepening concerns about the future of humanity living in an era of nuclear and environmental crisis.

If world's fairs have been mainstays, rather than just ornaments, of the modernizing world, how should they be understood? Efforts to resolve that question have cut across academic disciplines as historians, social scientists, and cultural studies scholars have focused their expertise on those amazing events. Although we risk oversimplifying the current debate about how to understand world's fairs, we find it useful to think in terms of six schools of thought.

The first may be termed the cultural hegemony school. Producer centered, it examines world's fairs largely through the intentions of their organizers and managers. Two studies in this vein, Robert Rydell's *All the World's a Fair* and *World of Fairs*, draw on the ideas of Marxist theorist Antonio Gramsci and argue that world's fairs need to be understood as vehicles intended to win popular support for national imperial policies. Rydell's argument has been extended by Tony Bennett's *The Birth of the Museum*, an examination of international expositions and museums that draws on the insights of Gramsci and French philosopher Michel Foucault to argue that fairs, which Bennett calls "exhibitionary complexes," functioned to "win the hearts and minds" of a mass audience.[2]

Another more nuanced reading of how fairs attempted—and sometimes failed—to achieve the aims of their sponsors is Keith Walden's *Becoming Modern in Toronto: The Industrial Exhibition and the Shaping of a Late Victorian Culture*. That study serves as a bridge into the second school of thought about world's fairs, one that is more audience centered. Work in this vein is exemplified by Eric Breitbart's film about the 1904 St. Louis fair, *World on Display*, James Gilbert's *Perfect Cities*, Karal Ann Marling's *Blue Ribbon: A Social and Pictorial History of the Minnesota State Fair*, and Leslie Prosterman's *Ordinary Life, Festival Days*. Although the latter two works concentrate on state fairs, both Marling and Prosterman argue for a more complex evaluation of the way fairgoers "read" fairs and derive their own meanings from them. The argument is perhaps best illustrated with this analogy: as every teacher knows, despite the best of intentions, students will make their own meanings out of what we say in the classroom. So too

5

with fairs and fairgoers. Despite the intentions of exposition organizers to organize the experiences of fairgoers and, at least in the nineteenth and early twentieth centuries, to educate those visitors, they were not necessarily taken in by the ideological messages of the fairs' sponsors.[3]

The third school of thought, perhaps best considered the counterhegemony school, carries audience-centered arguments still further. While many scholars have argued that world's fairs grossly exploited people of color who were routinely displayed at expositions from the Victorian era through the middle of the twentieth century, scholars like Lester G. Moses in *Wild West Shows and the Images of American Indians, 1883–1933* argue that American Indians were often able to use world's fairs and Wild West shows to their own advantage. Through their performances and displays at fairs, people in positions of relative powerlessness in American society, including American women, were able to challenge dominant stereotypes affixed to them.[4]

A fourth school of thought has been advanced by anthropologist Burton Benedict in *The Anthropology of World's Fairs*. Benedict argues that world's fairs are modern-day potlatches, rituals of abundance and gift giving that usually end in the destruction of property and possessions. Building on Benedict's insights and drawing on the views of anthropologist Victor Turner, historian Warren Susman argues that early world's fairs were "liminal" events that ushered Americans across the threshold of modernity into a brave new world that prized values of consumerism and personality over those of production and character.[5]

A fifth school of thought, which is more documentary in focus, has opened windows on the technological, scientific, architectural, and urban planning dimensions of world's fairs. Classic works in this area are the studies by Eric Breitbart, Julie K. Brown, Eugene Ferguson, Robert Fox, John Findling and Kimberly Pelle, Neil Harris, Thomas Hines, David Nye, and Brigitte Schroeder-Gudehus and Anne Rasmussen.[6]

Finally, a sixth school of thought provides a perspective on fairs that has both academic and nonacademic foundations. From their very beginning world's fairs have produced a tradition of writing that includes official histories of fairs and popular magazine articles, as well as general histories like John Allwood's *The Great Exhibitions* and Alfred Heller's *World's Fairs and the End of Progress*, and novels like E. L. Doctorow's *World's Fair* and David Gelernter's *1939: The Lost World of the Fair*. Closely related to this celebration of fairs is a tradition of collecting world's fair memorabilia. Several collectors with passions for world's fairs have enlivened many world's fair studies, our own included. New York designer Larry Zim and postal clerk Edward Orth became world's fair aficionados and amassed extraordinary collections of world's fair objects (including stamps, books, tables, Ferris Wheel pincushions, photographs, posters, and pinball machines) that they bequeathed to the Smithsonian Institution. Some collectors, like Donald Larson, have donated their materials to libraries like the Henry Madden Library at California State University, Fresno. Other collectors, like Mitchell Wolfson Jr., have built museums to house their collections. Still others, like Frederic and Mary Megson from New Jersey, have made their vast collections of world's fair postcards accessible to scholars. Writers and collectors in this tradition, unlike more critically minded scholars, have captured and conveyed the excitement of world's fairs—something most academics have yet to do—and all of us who have studied world's fair history are deeply in their debt.[7]

So how should world's fairs be understood? Clearly, no consensus exists among scholars, but they seem to be moving toward a view that stresses the complex and often contradictory nature of fairs. That view sees expositions as arenas of debate about what they contribute to the cultural milieu of societies that have hosted them. In *Fair America* we will try to clarify that interpretation with particular emphasis on the relationship between American world's fairs and the American political economy since the end of the Civil War.

Our argument can be previewed as follows. American world's fairs extended and carried forward into the cultural realm the political efforts to reconstruct the United States after the Civil War. Political reunification of the North and the South was accomplished in 1877 with a compromise over the results of the 1876 election that guaranteed the Republican Party control of the presidency in exchange for the withdrawal of federal troops from the South. Political reunion may have been completed, but did the reconstruction of the American nation simply come to a close with a political compromise? The social and economic history of the ensuing Gilded Age suggests otherwise.

Layered into the bitter memories of the Civil War was the growing realization that the massive industrialization unleashed by the war was dividing Americans into hardening class lines. Lingering effects of the Panic of 1873 led to the violence of the 1877 railroad strikes. The economy recovered somewhat in the 1880s, but not sufficiently in the eyes of many workers, some of whom turned to radical and reformist political alternatives like Socialism and Populism. With a growing number of middle-class Americans, including children of the Civil War generation, wondering if warfare between regions had been fought and won only to pave the way for warfare between social classes, America's political leaders and economic elites sought to win public approval for their visions of America's future. How could that approval be earned in an era before electronic media? One ready answer presented itself in the form of the thriving world's fair movement that was sweeping England and continental Europe in the wake of the successful 1851 Crystal Palace Exhibition. Like the Crystal Palace Exhibition, the fairs that were staged in its aftermath served to stave off political unrest at home and to build support for specific national imperial policies. The success of those fairs, especially the 1867 Paris Exhibition and 1873 Vienna Exhibition, led American nationalists to imagine that world's fairs were ideally suited to their needs, and they won the support of the U.S. government for the 1876 Philadelphia Centennial International Exhibition and the 1884–85 New Orleans World's Industrial and Cotton Centennial Exposition. So impressive were those fairs that when the four-hundredth anniversary of Columbus's landfall in the New World appeared on the horizon, Congress agreed to lend federal support for an even larger and more impressive world's fair in Chicago. That fair, the 1893 World's Columbian Exposition, was supposed to send a signal to Americans and to the rest of the world that the American nation had been rebuilt and that American civilization now rivaled anything Europe had to offer. But in the midst of that spectacle the bottom fell out of the American economy.

Appreciate the context. Internationally, the Paris Commune in 1871 had represented a direct challenge to industrial capitalism. Domestically, the Haymarket Massacre in 1886 and the Homestead Strike in 1892 had sent shock waves across the country. What would happen since the economy had entered a depression? What would be the future of the recently reunited United States? Would the pattern of social violence on a European scale be repeated in America?

Those questions demanded answers, and the responses took visible form in the world's fairs that spread across the United States—in Atlanta (1895), Nashville (1897), Omaha (1898), Buffalo (1901), St. Louis (1904), Portland

(1905), Jamestown (1907), Seattle (1909), San Francisco (1915), and San Diego (1915–16). Each of those fairs represented one thread in a web of expositions, and each sought to distill and to reconfigure crucial components of the nationalizing synthesis that came into view at the 1893 World's Columbian Exposition. That synthesis had two major components. The first component, which was essentially economic, entailed convincing an American mass audience that the future progress of the United States depended on overseas economic expansion and, if necessary, on extending America's political and military influence to secure economic ends. The second component, which was essentially racial, involved winning the support of white Americans, regardless of social class, for a view of the world that held that progress toward civilization could be understood in terms of allegedly innate racial characteristics.

That nationalizing synthesis was not without opposition. At the turn of the century, in the aftermath of the Spanish-American War, many Americans supported the cause of anti-imperialism, arguing that the government's quest for an overseas empire ran counter to America's longstanding commitment to political self-determination. Furthermore, African Americans and middle-class white women fought, and sometimes won, intense battles with exposition authorities over the ways they were represented at fairs. Other avenues of resistance were opened along world's fair midways when people who were put on display in ethnological villages as racial types insisted on being recognized as fully human, and when the strains of ragtime were first heard as counterpoints to patriotic airs blaring from bandstands on the main exposition grounds.

Fluid and restive, like American society itself, the contents of world's fairs always threatened to spill over and to subvert the intentions of their sponsors. But world's fair authorities were up to the challenges posed by the complexities and contradictions of the medium. The presence of unruly bodies along world's fair midways only seemed to heighten the sense of urgency they brought to bear on trying to discipline the larger body politic. Those disciplinary efforts came into particularly sharp relief at the 1893 World's Columbian Exposition in Chicago, where world's fair authorities turned the dedication ceremonies of their fair into a vehicle for carrying the Pledge of Allegiance—complete with a formal, military-style salute in its original version—into the nation's schools.

Nationalizing efforts like the Pledge of Allegiance and countless patriotic

World's fairs inspired American nationalism as this postcard sold at the Jamestown Tercentenary Exposition in
1907 demonstrates. (Photo courtesy of John E. Findling)

celebrations organized in conjunction with forty years of world's fairs
played a central role in reconstructing American political culture after the
Civil War and no doubt helped to underpin popular support for the decision by the U.S. government to enter World War I. But that war, fought
among so-called civilized nations, called into question the very values associated with progress and brought that optimistic era to an ironic and tragic
close.

In the 1920s, with much of Europe in ruins, European national governments, seeking ways to rebuild popular faith in their own national and imperial policies, once again turned to the world's fair medium and launched a series of expositions that embraced new, modernistic principles of architecture and design. In the United States, with the economy riding a high tide, interest in world's fairs waned. A world's fair held in Philadelphia to celebrate the sesquicentennial of American independence from England was one of the great failures in the history of world's fairs. But just when the United States seemed poised to fulfill the utopian predictions of exposition promoters in the decades before World War I, the American—and, indeed, global—economy crashed.

In the early 1930s the United States was facing its worst crisis since the Civil War. Globally, capitalism was facing its worst crisis ever. Confronted once again with the problem of shoring up popular faith in both the American political and economic systems, leading political, business, and intellectual authorities pumped new life—and lots of money—into the world's fair medium. Between 1933 and 1940 world's fairs again spanned the United States. Chicago (1933–34), San Diego (1935–36), Dallas (1936), Cleveland (1936–37), San Francisco (1939–40), and New York (1939–40) all hosted significant fairs. Some fairs, like the Century of Progress Exposition in Chicago, sought to divert attention away from the Great Depression by reminding Americans of past accomplishments; others, like the New York World's Fair, looked to the future by promising a better world of tomorrow. In all of America's depression era fairs, the dominant theme continued to be America's national progress toward a future utopia, but that theme contained a shift in emphasis. Progress, in addition to its other definitions, now meant increased consumer spending as world's fair sponsors tried to persuade Americans that they had to set aside older values such as thrift and restraint and become consumers of America's factory and farm products. By rebuilding America's domestic market, so the argument ran, consuming citizens could hasten America's economic recovery and put the United States back on track toward fulfilling its utopian potential. That primary message of those fairs was endorsed by President Franklin Delano Roosevelt and built into his New Deal administration's active participation in world's fairs, which once again played a key role in the reconstruction of the American nation-state during a crisis.

America's depression era fairs contained another message. Those exposi-

Decks of cards featuring world's fair buildings or logos were popular souvenirs at nearly every world's fair. This card shows the German pavilion at the 1893 World's Columbian Exposition. (Photo courtesy of John E. Findling)

tions also encouraged Americans to place their faith in the ability of scientists and engineers to design the world of tomorrow. Nowhere did that idea find clearer expression than in the motto of the Hall of Science at the Century of Progress Exposition: "Science Finds; Industry Applies; Man Conforms."

As ennobling and forward-looking as that idea may have seemed in the 1930s, it jolted the senses a decade later once the American public realized that science and science-based industries had helped to usher in the brave new world of nuclear/ecological crisis that defines the human condition at the beginning of the twenty-first century. After World War II, as the nuclear arms race between the Soviet Union and the United States, as well as a series of ecological disasters, contributed to deepening doubts about the future, a third generation of world's fairs mushroomed around the world. Some, like the 1958 Brussels Universal Exposition, with its towering Atomium, denied that nuclear energy posed a threat to humanity; others, like the 1970 Japan World Exposition in Osaka, held out hope for "Progress and Harmony for Mankind." Following the victory of the Allies in World War II and the creation of the United Nations, all postwar fairs proclaimed the existence of one world and a common humanity. But that declaration also masked the constant presence of the cold war and subtly advanced what historian Eric Hobsbawm has called "the new supranational restructuring of the globe" and the globalization of horrifically exploitative forms of corporate capitalism. In marked contrast to pre–World War I world's fairs, fairs in the post–World War II era, continuing a process that was in evidence at expositions between the two world wars, have been dominated by pavilions that represent the interests of transnational corporations. Whether this still-evolving generation of recent fairs will reconstruct—or reinvent by redirecting—those national loyalties that were so carefully cultivated by early world's fair authorities remains to be seen. It also remains to be seen whether the medium of the world's fair, now wedded more firmly than ever to the interests of transnational corporations, will suggest solutions for the nuclear/ecological disaster that may await us all, or whether world's fairs in the twenty-first century will leave us whistling in the dark.[8]

1
FAIRS IN THE AGE OF
INDUSTRIALISM'S ADVANCE

*O*n May 1, 1851, Queen Victoria confided to her journal that "this is one of the greatest and most glorious days of our lives, with which, to my pride and joy, the name of my dearly beloved Albert is for ever associated! . . . [B]efore we neared the Crystal Palace, the sun shone and gleamed upon the gigantic edifice, upon which the flags of every nation were flying. . . . The sight as we came to the center . . . facing the beautiful crystal fountain was magic and impressive. The tremendous cheering, the joy expressed in every face, the vastness of the building, and my beloved husband, the creator of this peace festival . . . , all this was indeed moving and a day to live for ever."[1]

The queen was writing about the opening ceremonies for the first great modern world's fair, the Crystal Palace Exhibition, also called more formally the Great Exhibition of the Works of Industry of All Nations, which was held in London's Hyde Park during the summer of 1851. Largely the work of the queen's consort, Prince Albert, and cultural reformer Henry Cole, the Crystal Palace Exhibition was in some ways a union of trade or industrial exhibitions, which had been known in France and England since the 1760s, and art exhibitions, also an eighteenth-century innovation. But the Crystal Palace moved far beyond those exhibitions, which often were held in crowded spaces, attracted relatively little public notice, and had few, if any, international dimensions.

What Prince Albert and Henry Cole had in mind was a much larger exhibition, one that would include the industrial achieve-

The Crystal Palace, shown here after it was moved to the London suburb of Sydenham, remained in use as a venue for trade shows and small fairs until it burned down in 1936. (Photo courtesy of John E. Findling)

ments of many nations, whose products could then be matched against those of the British. Because Britain was far and away the world's leading industrial power at that time, Prince Albert and Henry Cole had little doubt that the comparisons would reflect favorably upon the host nation.

To house the exhibition, Joseph Paxton, a horticulturist and greenhouse builder, designed a stunning iron and glass structure 1,848 feet long and 408 feet wide, with an extension on the north side measuring 936 feet by 48 feet. The building covered nineteen acres and boasted nine hundred thousand square feet of glass. Because the glass panes and iron framework were prefabricated and interchangeable, the entire building was constructed in about six months. The Crystal Palace was a spectacular sight, lent its name to the exhibition, and served as a model for the buildings of many later world's fairs. Moreover, the Crystal Palace used the highest level of technology available in 1850 and, in doing so, served as the perfect site for an exhibition that focused on the finest achievements of the industrializing world.[2]

Even Queen Victoria seemed more enchanted with the machinery at the Crystal Palace than with other aspects of the fair. She kept a special journal to record her thoughts and feelings about the Crystal Palace, which she visited many times, and on one occasion she wrote, "Went to the machinery part, where we remained two hours, and which is excessively interesting and instructive. . . . What used to be done by hand and used to take several months doing is now accomplished in a few instants [sic] by the most beautiful machinery." While not everyone agreed with the queen—William Morris, who believed strongly in the virtue of handcrafted items, was appalled at the extravagant machinery on display, which he thought degraded working people—clearly she was right on the mark. All subsequent fairs of that period showcased the latest advances in industrial and mechanical technology, and the beautiful machinery was usually a prime attraction for visitors.[3]

The Crystal Palace Exhibition attracted more than six million visitors during its five-and-a-half-month run and showed a profit of £186,000. After the exhibition closed in October 1851, the Crystal Palace was taken down and rebuilt at Sydenham, a London suburb. There, for the next eighty-five years, it served as an exhibition and entertainment center until it burned in a spectacular nighttime fire on November 30, 1936. But by then the legacy of the Crystal Palace was assured. Following upon its success, some sixty world's fairs were held before 1915 in locales as diverse as Kingston, Jamaica; Hobart, Tasmania; and Dublin, Ireland. Of those, nearly twenty took place in the United States.[4]

The United States had contributed extensive displays to the Crystal Palace Exhibition, impressing the British with American industrial and manufacturing prowess. Cyrus McCormick's reapers and Samuel Colt's revolvers attracted particular notice in the British press as evidence of America's technological progress. Many Americans visited the London fair. It was not surprising, then, that one of them, Edward Riddle, an auctioneer from Massachusetts, returned home and contacted P. T. Barnum, the showman and later circus king, hoping to interest the ambitious Barnum in lending his name to an American version of the Crystal Palace. Barnum was not interested at the time, but other New Yorkers were, and in January 1852 the city granted them a five-year lease for a parcel of land at what was called Reservoir Square (now Bryant Park, next to the New York Public Library) to be used as a fair site. The city specified that the building must be constructed of glass and iron and that the admission charge be no more than fifty cents. The federal government cooperated by classifying the building as a bonded warehouse, which apparently solved foreign exhibitors' problems with U.S. Customs and facilitated contact with foreign nations.[5]

Mired in the worsening problems of the sectional crisis and not convinced of the nation-building potential of a great world's fair, the federal government, however, was not willing to sponsor the New York fair, as had been the case in London, where a royal commission had managed the Crystal Palace. Lack of federal support, reflecting a lack of support from Southerners, did not deter New Yorkers. A competition was held for the building design, and Joseph Paxton submitted a design, but it was rejected because it did not fit the square shape of the site. Charles Gildemeister, a New York architect, and George Carstensen, a Dane, won the competition with a design that used the same structural principles as Paxton's Crystal Palace with one exception. Instead of using glass in the roof, which let in too much light, the architects decided on wood. Unfortunately, the wooden roof leaked. A nice touch, however, was the installation in the dome of thirty-two stained glass windows, showing the coats of arms of the United States and its thirty-one states.

Because of building delays, the fair opened three months late, in July 1853, but President Franklin Pierce attended the opening ceremony to express his hope that the fair would help reunite a divided nation. It did not. Attendance was disappointing, and Barnum was brought in for a second season to try to recoup some of the $100,000 lost during the inaugural season. He could not work his magic, however, and by the final closing in November 1854, the fair's losses totaled some $340,000. When the New York Crystal Palace burned to the ground in 1858, a local critic wrote, "So bursts a bubble rather noteworthy in the annals of New York. To be accurate, the bubble burst some years ago, and this catastrophe merely annihilates the apparatus that generated it."[6]

As an effort to inspire Americans with a sense of nationalism, the New York Crystal Palace Exhibition failed. Twenty-three years would pass before another world's fair would be held in America. But fairs continued to flourish in Europe, with London (1862), Paris (1855 and 1867), and Vienna (1873) hosting, in turn, the largest as promoters of each fair tried to outshine their predecessors in expressing the host country's nationalistic spirit and

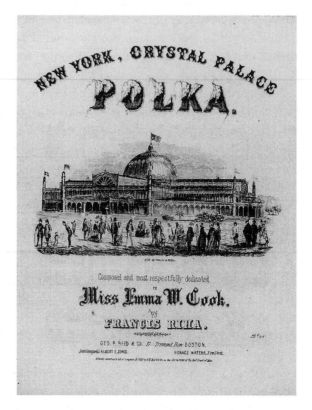

They were not dancing the polka when the New York Crystal Palace burned down in 1858. Special music was composed for many world's fairs but seldom achieved lasting popularity. "Meet Me in St. Louis, Louis," composed for the 1904 fair, is an exception. (Photo courtesy of the Larson Collection, Sanoian Special Collections Library, Henry Madden Library, California State University, Fresno)

economic development. Meanwhile, Americans fought the Civil War, tried to reconstruct their nation, and began to experience the coming of a full-fledged industrial revolution to their cities.

After the Civil War, a combination of forces propelled the United States into the industrial age. Clever capitalists exploited the discovery of great deposits of natural resources, notably coal, oil, and iron ore. They invested in the technological advances like railroads and telegraphs that significantly increased production rates and took advantage of both capital and labor, as well as a noninterfering federal government, to build giant industries in oil, steel, railroads, meat packing, flour milling, and many other enterprises. The new wealth of those capitalists became the object of conspicuous display in mansions that dotted the American landscape and inspired Mark Twain to label the era the Gilded Age. Their interest in staging conspicuous displays of wealth also motivated their interest in the Victorian era's most extravagant exhibitionary form—the world's fair—but with this twist. The wealthy supporters of world's fairs were interested not only in showing off their private wealth but also in investing that wealth in a medium that they believed would help rebuild—literally reconstruct—the American nation after four years of bloody civil war. Inspired by the nation-building examples of European exhibitions, they determined to use the medium of the world's fair to hasten the transformation of the recently reunited states into the United States.

What seemed like a good idea in the late 1860s suddenly in the early 1870s acquired a sense of urgency. In 1873 a financial panic triggered the first in a series of industrial depressions that would recur with some degree of regularity between the era of Reconstruction and World War II. With contemporary political revolutions in Europe very much on their minds, America's budding corporate leaders and their allies in the government determined to use the medium of the world's fair as a means to restore public faith in the legitimacy of their authority to direct American society. The 1876 Philadelphia Centennial Exhibition gave them a golden opportunity to put their convictions to the test.

Planning for the Centennial International Exhibition, as it was formally known, began in 1871, when Congress authorized the creation of a centennial commission. There was never any question that Philadelphia would be the site; indeed the original idea for the exhibition came from John L. Campbell, a Wabash College professor, in a lecture at the Smithsonian Institution in 1864 and then in a letter to the mayor of Philadelphia in 1866.

Most of the financing and fiscal responsibility for the exhibition fell to Philadelphia's elite, who then went on to organize and to manage the event. Such was the case with all the early world's fairs: they were the creations of the host city's social and financial upper class, who propagated a particular view of the world that insisted on the presumed fact of Anglo-Saxon racial superiority as a way to unite whites, regardless of social class, at the expense of people defined as racially determined "others."[7]

By 1876 fairs had grown too large to be contained in one building. At the Philadelphia Centennial International Exhibition, the Horticultural Hall housed elaborate exhibits related to agriculture. (Photo courtesy of John E. Findling)

In 1873 the U.S. Centennial Commission received the right to use 450 acres in Philadelphia's Fairmount Park, the largest urban park in the country, and hired Hermann J. Schwartzmann to design the fair. Schwartzmann, a young architect and engineer who had emigrated from Germany, realized that the projected size of the fair—the largest fair held to date—would make it impossible to utilize just one building, as had been the case in past fairs. His plan, therefore, called for six major buildings, as well as smaller pavilions for states and foreign countries, and many smaller structures to be used for restaurants and other commercial and support services. That format became the standard for all the great world's fairs that followed.

Among the principal buildings, the Main Building, at 1,880 feet long by 464 feet wide, approached the size of the Crystal Palace in London, and Machinery Hall was nearly as large. One of the other principal buildings, Memorial Hall, was designed as a permanent structure and housed an ex-

The cavernous interior of Machinery Hall at the 1876
Philadelphia Centennial International Exhibition showcased thousands of industrial products. (Photo courtesy of
the Larson Collection, Sanoian Special Collections Library,
Henry Madden Library, California State University, Fresno)

tensive fine arts exhibition. Although fine art had been displayed at earlier
fairs, the Centennial International Exhibition was the first fair at which a
major exhibit hall was devoted to painting and sculpture. Most subsequent
fairs would follow suit and include a fine arts pavilion in their plans.

Most of the construction was completed by the opening ceremonies on
May 10, 1876, and visitors thronged to see the dazzling exhibits. As had hap-
pened at London's Crystal Palace Exhibition, the machinery awed the fairgoers. In the words of Ben Beverly, a fictional Chicago lawyer visiting the
fair, "it is impossible to convey any adequate idea of the extent and richness
in [the Main Building] of the exposition. . . . We see a vast room, about
one-third of a mile in length, and three hundred and fifty feet wide, filled

LOST IN WONDER.

Fairgoers were often awestruck by the multitude of new inventions and products displayed at early world's fairs. (Photo courtesy of the Larson Collection, Sanoian Special Collections Library, Henry Madden Library, California State University, Fresno)

with the finest products of man's skill and industry, from all parts of the world." The centerpiece of the fair was the gigantic Corliss engine, located in Machinery Hall, but both that building and the Main Building were also filled with thousands of manufactured products from the United States and other countries, with American products occupying the greatest amount of space. As had been the case at the Crystal Palace Exhibition twenty-five years before, America's industrial and agricultural prowess impressed most foreign visitors, thus giving a boost to American foreign trade, then in its infancy. One visitor who was less than impressed was John Lewis, a native of England living in New York and working in a wholesale grocery business. In a letter to his brother back in England, Lewis wrote:

The great Corliss engine that drives most of the machinery of the building—that's a fraud. There are plenty of larger Engines than that. It is imposing on account of its position and its having double beams and a large flywheel. . . . There is 2 cylinders, each I think 38 in. and the stroke is not long. Now there are plenty of cylinders of 80, 90 and up to 108 in.—which must be of many times the power of the Corliss machines.[8]

The organizers of the Philadelphia Centennial International Exhibition believed that the exhibits demonstrated that the future growth and progress of the United States (and, implicitly, the entire world) would come about only under the guidance of the superior Anglo-Saxon race. That notion was suggested in the Main Building and Machinery Hall where the foreign exhibits were arranged on a racial basis, with the more Anglo-Saxon nations awarded more central locations.[9]

The federal government entrusted much of its participation at the Centennial Exhibition (and most subsequent major fairs of that era) to the Smithsonian Institution and its staff of anthropologists and ethnologists. For the Centennial Exhibition, the Smithsonian, under the direction of its secretary, Joseph Henry, decided to focus its efforts on American Indian exhibits that would represent the Indians as primitive or savage counterpoints to forward-looking, so-called civilized white Americans. The American public generally assumed in 1876 that the Indians were quickly disappearing and probably would be extinct or fully merged into mainstream America within the next century. Those displays did nothing to prepare visitors for the newspaper headlines that summer announcing that Indians assembled at the Little Bighorn River in far-off Montana had annihilated Lt. Col. George A. Custer's command. But those exhibits certainly helped provide a rationalization for the extreme violence that the federal government deployed in the ensuing wars against Indians living in the upper plains.[10]

Precisely because cultural representations were so powerful and seemingly definitive, they became a major source of controversy at the Centennial Exhibition. Some women, for instance, were pleased that the fair's directors had relegated examples of women's arts and inventions to a separate Women's Building, which many thought represented a significant step toward equality and the right to vote. Not so pleased, however, were Susan B. Anthony and other leaders of the suffrage movement, who embarrassed fair managers by presenting a scroll containing the Declaration of the Rights of Women to a surprised Vice President Thomas W. Ferry, "pale as he will be when dead," during the special July 4 ceremonies at the fairgrounds.[11]

African Americans, who might have hoped for some recognition of their

23

American Indian exhibits, such as these totem poles from
the Philadelphia Centennial International Exhibition, con-
firmed many visitors' beliefs that Indians were uncivilized.
(Photo courtesy of the Larson Collection, Sanoian Special
Collections Library, Henry Madden Library, California
State University, Fresno)

accomplishments since emancipation from slavery only a decade earlier,
were equally disappointed. None worked on the construction of the fair
buildings, and only a few held menial jobs during the fair. No space was set
aside for the accomplishments of blacks, and black women were shut out
of the Women's Building. On opening day police officials even tried to pre-
vent Frederick Douglass, the most prominent black in the United States,
from taking his place on the speakers' stand. Suffice it to say, the Centennial Exhibition not only reflected the politics of racial discrimination but
also endorsed them.[12]

When it closed on November 10, 1876, the Centennial Exhibition had
attracted nearly ten million visitors out of a total U.S. population of forty-six

million. Although the fair and its investors lost money, most critics felt that it had been successful in restoring national pride and encouraging the recovery of American business after the Panic of 1873. The cultural success of the exhibition, seen in the popularity of its exhibits, mechanical and ethnological alike, and the friendly reception in the press launched the world's fair movement in the United States. Over the next forty years major fairs took place in Chicago, Omaha, Buffalo, St. Louis, San Diego, and San Francisco, while smaller fairs were held in many other cities, particularly in the South. In different ways all of those fairs supported the proposition that the advance of the American industrial economy, as directed by an Anglo-Saxon elite, was synonymous with national progress.[13]

By the late 1870s southern businessmen, along with their northern suppliers, brokers, and customers, realized that the economic recovery of the South would never be completed until the region developed a more industrialized and diversified economy. Although southern states had not been well represented at the Centennial International Exhibition in Philadelphia, Southerners who attended were impressed with the grandeur of the buildings, the scope of the exhibits, and, most important, the potential for business expansion that international expositions seemed to offer.

Atlanta's business leaders, including banker Samuel Inman and newspaperman W. A. Hemphill, were the first in the South to organize a world's fair. They formed an organizing committee in April 1880, and H. I. Kimball, a well-known local politician and civic booster, became the fair's director general. While Kimball raised money and handled publicity for the fair, Edward Atkinson of Boston, a cotton trader with extensive southern business connections, laid out the buildings for the fair and suggested that foreign exhibitors be invited. The site for the fair, Oglethorp Park, was large enough to accommodate the four principal exhibit buildings, as well as a real cotton field.

During its three-month run, from October through December 1881, the International Cotton Exposition attracted 290,000 visitors and proved a great success in promoting the sale of farm implements and machinery. Exhibitors came from thirty-three states and seven foreign countries. Although the fair itself closed with a modest financial loss, most organizers no doubt felt that the stimulus to business was well worth the price. Moreover, the success of the Atlanta fair prompted business leaders in both Louisville and

New Orleans to begin planning their own events. The Louisville fair, known as the Southern Exposition, was a rather modest effort that opened with a three-month run in 1883 and turned into an annual event that ran through 1887. Designed to encourage the use of Louisville as a major transportation link between the North and the South, the Southern Exposition was notable in that it succeeded without any direct governmental aid.[14]

New Orleans called its 1884–85 fair the World's Industrial and Cotton Centennial Exposition, and it was a much more ambitious project than its predecessors in Atlanta or Louisville. For example, the Main Building covered more space than the entire Atlanta site in Oglethorp Park and boasted a music hall that seated eleven thousand, with a stage large enough to accommodate six hundred performers. Despite the opportunities for extravagant music productions, the New Orleans fair was concerned with business and the recovery of the southern economy. The U.S. Congress, interested in improving the national economy, endorsed the New Orleans fair and directed the appropriate federal government agencies to help stage the event in conjunction with the city of New Orleans and the National Cotton Planters Association. The "centennial" in its name referred to the anniversary of the first U.S. cotton shipment to Europe, and one of the goals of this fair was to encourage farmers and businessmen in the Mississippi River valley to use the port of New Orleans. In addition, outward-looking Southerners saw the potential of Latin American markets and discussed the possibility of the United States displacing Great Britain as the leading commercial nation doing business in that part of the world.

Although the planners of the New Orleans fair worked hard to produce a grandiose exposition, they were plagued with problems from the beginning. Bad weather, negative publicity at the beginning of the fair because of the many unfinished buildings, and the relatively remote location hurt attendance and led to significant financial liabilities, with losses estimated at $470,000. Attendance, forecast to be 4 million, reached only 1.2 million, and the city's economy showed little noticeable improvement.[15]

The southern fair movement might have ended after the New Orleans fiasco had it not been for the glamorous and culturally successful World's Columbian Exposition in Chicago in 1893. Despite the economic depression that swept across the country in 1893, Atlanta business leaders took heart from the Chicago exposition and staged the Cotton States and International Exposition in 1895. By that time foreign trade had grown in importance in American economic thinking; many people thought that increasing foreign trade would pull the nation out of the depression.

Once again business leaders saw Latin American markets as the most likely for American business to penetrate, and so the purpose of the fair was to encourage southern textile manufacturers to develop products suitable for those foreign markets. Before the fair, Isaac W. Avery, a lawyer and newspaperman, was sent by the U.S. Department of State to South America to publicize both the fair and the desire of U.S. manufacturers to enter the Latin American marketplace. While some Latin American leaders feared that increased U.S. trade would inevitably lead to U.S. political or military intervention, Avery did his best to convince them that their economic interests would be best served by the emerging new industries of the South.

The Cotton States and International Exposition in Atlanta drew 780,000 visitors in its three-month run and captured national headlines. The *New York Times* reported in December 1895, just before the fair closed, that the positive image this fair had communicated was "infinitely greater than was expected by even the most enthusiastic and patriotic of its managers." The author of an illustrated history of the exposition published in 1896 claimed that the fair "stimulated public spirit with a new ambition for commercial greatness" and helped to generate interest in a Nicaraguan canal and friendly relations with "Southern countries." The Atlanta fair's success also gave a boost to the planners of the Tennessee Centennial Exposition, held in Nashville in 1897.[16]

By 1897, with much of the country experiencing an economic recovery, organizers of the Nashville fair, while not ignoring the economic imperative of a world's fair and the chance to promote Tennessee as an "inviting field for the investment of capital," also saw the fair as an opportunity to "rekindle patriotism and [the] appreciation of [our] often overlooked history." They took a great deal of care with the design of the fair buildings, of which the most important was a replica of the Parthenon of Athens, which was intended to identify the spirit of the New South with the spirit of democracy. Inside the replica of the Parthenon and the other buildings, the usual array of domestic and foreign industrial products and exhibits of natural resources attracted 1.2 million visitors, including President William McKinley, whose enthusiasm for fairs was almost unbounded.[17]

Following the Nashville exposition, two more fairs took place in the South before World War I. Between December 1901 and June 1902,

The Jamestown Tercentenary Exposition of 1907 reflected a strong militaristic sense as evidenced by this postcard showing ships of the American navy. (Photo courtesy of John E. Findling)

Charleston, South Carolina, hosted an exposition with the awkward name of the South Carolina, Inter-State and West Indian Exposition. There were no historical anniversaries to celebrate at Charleston; the principal object was to promote the city as a port from which to carry on a profitable trade to and from the West Indies. America's acquisition of Puerto Rico and a protectorate over Cuba in the Spanish-American War signaled a new interest in the economic potential of the Caribbean. Five years later the Jamestown Tercentenary Exposition took place near Hampton Roads, Virginia, not far from the historic location of the original Jamestown settlement. At the urging of President Theodore Roosevelt, the Jamestown exposition included substantial military and naval displays as part of the festivities. Despite the support of that popular president, the fair failed financially. The $2.5 million loss was attributed to early negative publicity, a small local population, and the difficulty people had in getting to the Hampton Roads–Norfolk area. Of its nearly three million visitors, about half were admitted free.[18]

Southern fairs continued to feature the Smithsonian's anthropological displays. At the New Orleans fair, for example, Smithsonian anthropologists continued to develop the theme of Anglo-Saxon racial superiority, that time by suggesting a theory that races went through a sort of life span not unlike that of humans and that primitive races were in the earliest stage of their lives and thus needed protection and nurturing from the more advanced races. Comparisons were also made between so-called primitive races and criminals by displays of the small skulls and brains of each, alongside the larger skulls and brains of individuals who were considered to be more highly developed.[19]

Most southern fairs gave special attention to African Americans and developed so-called Negro departments and Negro pavilions to show the accomplishments of blacks, but the underlying idea was to demonstrate what good agricultural and industrial workers they were rather than to suggest a movement toward equality and upward social mobility. There was disagreement within the black community about whether, under those conditions, blacks should bother to participate. In general those who believed that some recognition was better than none at all prevailed. At the New Orleans exposition, for instance, blacks organized a Colored Department as part of the U.S. government display. Said to represent a new era for blacks, the exhibit included some sixteen thousand items, ranging from mechanical inventions to engravings of abolitionists. Under the emerging conditions of racial apartheid in the United States, having even a limited presence at expositions proved notable, or so some black leaders argued, because the fair afforded them a platform from which to make rhetorical demands for economic, social, and racial equality.

By the 1890s, with lynching becoming a way of life in the South, some African Americans, led by Booker T. Washington, principal of Tuskegee Institute, began to urge that blacks needed to de-emphasize their demands for civil rights and to insist instead on greater economic opportunities. Washington made his position clear in his famous Atlanta Compromise speech at the 1895 Cotton States and International Exposition in Atlanta. In his address he encouraged blacks to be satisfied with manual labor and to recognize the folly of striving for full social equality. Faced with the repression of the Jim Crow era (the *Plessy v. Ferguson* Supreme Court decision, legalizing "separate but equal" facilities for the races, was less than a year away), more and more black leaders were no longer happy with second-class citizenship. Washington's speech was criticized, as was participation in the fair's Negro Building (which exhibited black handiwork and was the only

Most southern fairs of this era relegated African American exhibits to a separate Negro Building such as this one at the Jamestown Tercentenary Exposition of 1907. (Photo courtesy of John E. Findling)

place on the fairgrounds where black visitors could purchase refreshments), for lending support to segregation in the American South. Would a boycott of the fair have been a better strategy for blacks to adopt? African Americans remained divided about the best course of action to pursue with respect to the "white cities" mushrooming across the United States in the wake of America's most important Victorian era exposition, the 1893 Chicago World's Columbian Exposition.[20]

In the early 1880s interest grew in staging a world's fair to celebrate the four-hundredth anniversary of Columbus's landfall in the New World in 1892. Early on, some Chicagoans began touting their city as a good location for such a fair because of its central location, railroad network, and reasonably temperate summer weather. New York, St. Louis, Philadelphia, and Washington, D.C., also launched campaigns to host the fair, with New York and St. Louis emerging as Chicago's most serious rivals.

In 1889 a group of prominent Chicago businessmen formed a citizens' committee to orchestrate Chicago's campaign for the fair, and similar groups were created in New York and St. Louis. New Yorkers argued that their city deserved the fair because it was the largest commercial center and port. Boosters in St. Louis promoted their city as even more centrally located than Chicago, with similar weather and accessibility.

The Chicago committee withstood New York's claim that its campaign was just the nonsense of a "windy city," which led to a popular nickname for the midwestern city. New York's fight to get the fair was weakened by factional quarreling among New York Republican leaders, but what probably convinced Congress, which made the final decision, to favor Chicago was the pledge by some of Chicago's wealthiest residents to commit $10 million to build and to manage the exposition. In April 1890 Congress voted to place the fair in Chicago and determined that it would be held in 1893 rather than 1892 because of the late date of the authorization.

Because congressmen still had questions about Chicago's ability to put on such a large undertaking, Congress created a special committee to oversee the preparations for the fair. That committee was to work in some manner with Chicago's local committee, but the relationship was never well defined, and conflict between the two groups threatened to disrupt the planning process. Late in 1890, however, a budget-minded Congress cut funding for its committee, thus leaving the local committee free to develop its own plans for the event.[21]

An important and difficult issue concerned the site for the exposition. Chicago had several large, unimproved parks that seemed suitable to some boosters, but others recoiled at the idea of that natural park land ruined by the roads and buildings of a fair. Others argued that a downtown site would be most convenient, but such a site would not have enough room for the many agricultural and livestock exhibits. Some members of the committee suggested an alternative plan: using a downtown site for the manufacturing and government exhibits and using Jackson Park, about eight miles south of downtown but easily accessible by either train or boat, for the farm-related exhibits. Finally, Frederick Law Olmsted, the eminent landscape designer who had drawn up plans for Chicago's park development earlier, was brought in; he helped convince the committee to site the entire exposition in Jackson Park, which would facilitate the implementation of his plan for that park.[22]

Chicagoans had other reasons for wanting to host the World's Columbian Exposition, as it came to be known. They wanted to celebrate the remarkable recovery the city had made from the devastating fire of 1871 and to overcome the blow to the city's reputation that followed the Haymarket Massacre of 1886, when several policemen had been killed or injured by a bomb at a labor rally. In the years after Haymarket, civic leaders built libraries, the Art Institute, and the University of Chicago as examples of high culture. The Auditorium Building, designed by Louis Sullivan and Dankmar Adler, was an acoustical wonder for theatrical production, and the Chicago Symphony, directed by Theodore Thomas, became one of the most outstanding orchestras in the country. The World's Columbian Exposition was the culmination of this cultural renaissance; no longer was Chicago the city that Rudyard Kipling had scorned: "Having seen it, I urgently desire never to see it again."[23]

To make certain that the rest of the country did not think of the World's Columbian Exposition as a "cattle show on the shores of Lake Michigan," as some in the press were suggesting, planners knew that they had to take care with the overall design of the fair. Moreover, they wanted to build a more impressive fair than the 1889 Paris Universal Exposition, which had featured the Eiffel Tower and an immense showing of French colonial possessions. Seeking a design for a tower that would outdo the Eiffel Tower, the *Chicago Tribune* sponsored a public competition. Many designs were submitted, including one for a tower shaped like a very large egg. None, however, was acceptable to the fair's board, and the signature structure for the exposition turned out to be the 264-foot-high wheel designed by engineer George Ferris.[24]

The design of the exposition buildings was entrusted to the Chicago firm of Burnham and Root, which had been active in the city's growth since the 1870s. The principals, Daniel Burnham and John W. Root, had helped to determine Jackson Park as the site, and Burnham became chief of construction while Root became supervising architect. Olmsted accepted the post of consulting landscape architect and with Henry S. Codman, his assistant, worked closely with Burnham and Root. They settled on a site plan in which the principal buildings composed a Court of Honor situated around an imposing formal lagoon. Other buildings would be constructed in a more parklike setting around a body of water featuring an island.

Because of the large size of the site—some 686 acres—and the number of buildings, Burnham and Root decided to assemble a team of architects to design the principal buildings. Among the team members were some of

The most prominent structure at the 1893 World's Columbian Exposition in Chicago was the Ferris Wheel on the Midway Plaisance. (Reprinted from *Official Views of the World's Columbian Exposition* [Chicago: Gravure Co., 1893])

the leading names in American architecture: from the east Richard Morris Hunt, George B. Post, and the firm of McKim, Mead, and White, and from Chicago Solon S. Beman, William L. Jenney, and the firm of Adler and Sullivan. Together they would turn the fair into a laboratory for the City Beautiful movement, a major component in the agenda of the era's Progressive reformers who sought to beautify American cities and to make them more efficient.

The fair's eastern architects met in New York in December 1890. Bowing to Burnham's wish that the design be unified, they adopted neoclassical styles and a common cornice height for the buildings around the Court of Honor. That decision was popular despite Louis Sullivan's later complaint that it set the cause of American architecture back by fifty years. Critics saw the formal, distinguished style as one that would generate the civic respect the fair board desired while still offering opportunities for creativity and diversity.

The Court of Honor at the World's Columbian Exposition dazzled visitors with its neoclassical architecture. Shown here is the U.S. Government Building, which formed part of the Court of Honor. (Reprinted from *Official Views of the World's Columbian Exposition* [Chicago: Gravure Co., 1893])

Tragedy struck in January 1891. While the eastern architects were visiting Chicago, Root died of pneumonia. His death was a blow to the project because he was generally regarded as more imaginative and creative than Burnham. For example, Root had urged that the fair buildings be painted in a variety of colors; after his death, the architects decided to paint everything around the Court of Honor a dazzling white, which gave rise to the nickname the "White City" for the exposition.[25]

The Court of Honor was situated at the south end of the Jackson Park site. To the north was an area of smaller fair buildings as well as state and foreign pavilions. Notable there was the Fine Arts Building, which for fire safety reasons was the only permanent building on the site and is now the Museum of Science and Industry. Also in that group of buildings was Adler and Sullivan's Transportation Building, with its arched golden entryway adding a refreshing splash of color to the White City.

At the World's Columbian Exposition Louis Sullivan impressed architectural critics and annoyed fair managers with his distinctive design highlighted by a golden arch entrance of the Transportation Building. (Reprinted from *Official Views of the World's Columbian Exposition* [Chicago: Gravure Co., 1893])

To the west, the Midway Plaisance, an entertainment area, extended along a wide thoroughfare for twelve blocks. The architects of the fair included this area after the success of a privately operated entertainment area that had sprung up next to the Philadelphia Centennial International Exhibition. That operation had offered types of entertainment that offended the fair management, which had no control over its activities. On the Midway, as it was known (probably because no one knew how to pronounce "plaisance"), stood the giant Ferris Wheel, an array of exotic shows from faraway places, including Algerian women doing the *danse du ventre*, or belly dance, and some native villages, where the mostly white fairgoers could take comfort in observing the so-called primitive and savage races work and play in a social Darwinian setting that seemed to validate current ideas about racial hierarchies.[26]

Construction of the fair buildings began in July 1891 and was not quite

LITTLE EGYPT

Newsboy

327

NEW YORK.

North African exotic dancers hootchie-kootchied their way into the hearts of thousands of male fairgoers at the World's Columbian Exposition in 1893, although one named Little Egypt may have been just a publicist's invention. (Photo courtesy of the Larson Collection, Sanoian Special Collections Library, Henry Madden Library, California State University, Fresno)

finished when the fair opened May 1, 1893. Bad winter weather and occasional labor disputes took their toll on the building schedule, even though Burnham pushed the workers mercilessly. Not much more than half the work was completed by October 21, 1892, the day designated as Dedication Day because it was the precise anniversary of Columbus's first sighting of the New World. The elaborate ceremonies attracted one hundred thousand people to the Manufactures and Liberal Arts Building (the largest at the fair). There they heard a five thousand–voice chorus and plenty of platitudinous speeches, including one given by Bertha Honoré Palmer, the unquestioned leader of Chicago society and the president of the Board of Lady Managers at the fair.

Equally impressive ceremonies took place away from the fairgrounds in public schools around the country. For the occasion of the fair's dedication, Francis J. Bellamy, an editor of a popular children's magazine, *The Youth's Companion*, wrote the words for "the salute to the flag," now the Pledge of Allegiance. Intended to promote the fair and underscore its significance as a nationalizing event, the Pledge of Allegiance would become one of the fair's most important legacies.[27]

Once the fair opened, the Court of Honor was, for most visitors, a sight they would always remember. Five gigantic neoclassical buildings, all seemingly connected by their equal cornice heights, surrounded the lagoon in which two huge sculptures seemed almost to float. Daniel Chester French's Statue of the Republic was a classical allegory of the United States, while Frederick William MacMonnies's Columbian Fountain paid homage to the explorer whose voyage the fair was honoring. With its multiple manifestations of "civilization," it was somehow fitting that this setting served as the general backdrop for historian Frederick Jackson Turner's famous address about the end of the frontier period in American history, which he delivered to a meeting of professional historians held in conjunction with the fair.

The Administration Building, Richard Morris Hunt's contribution, dominated the west end of the court with its large black and gold dome, while George B. Post's Manufactures and Liberal Arts Building, at 787 feet by 1,687 feet, was the largest building in the world at that time. After the fair, critics, such as the notable Montgomery Schuyler, agreed that the architectural unity of the buildings around the Court of Honor contributed much to the aesthetic success of the fair. Schuyler also praised the landscape plan, while other critics were impressed with the planning that had gone into making the World's Columbian Exposition a self-sufficient city complete with all the necessary services, including extraordinary attention to public sanitation. It was not surprising, then, that one of the fair's legacies was the spur that it gave to the city planning movement; in Chicago

Burnham began working in that area after the fair and in 1909 published his *Plan of Chicago*, which served as the basis for the city's development until the 1950s.[28]

Anthropology was one of the main sciences exhibited at the World's Columbian Exposition. Frederic Ward Putnam of Harvard University headed the fair's anthropology section, with the assistance of Franz Boas. Although many of the so-called living anthropology exhibits were on the Midway, Putnam and Boas tried to make them educational, but they were frequently frustrated by Sol Bloom, the young impresario who brought entertainment to the Midway, based on what he had seen in Paris in 1889. While Putnam and the fair board treated race in a traditional hegemonic manner, placing the advanced technology of the Anglo-Saxon nations at the center of the fairgrounds and the displays of the lesser races farther away from the center, Bloom's Midway rejoiced in the opportunities to make money from its commercialized exoticism. On much of the Midway, visitors saw ethnic and racial diversity meant to entertain, titillate, and educate. The distinctions often blurred, however, as Bloom's object was to make money. Each exhibit and show on the Midway had its own admission charge, in contrast to the main part of the fairgrounds where a single fifty-cent admission allowed visitors to see everything.

Although the boundaries between education and entertainment may have dissolved along the Midway, fairgoers who wanted to see a more scholarly display of anthropology and ethnology could visit Putnam and Boas's exhibits in the Anthropology Building, located at the southern end of the fairgrounds, or the Smithsonian's exhibits, found in both the U.S. Government Building and the Woman's Building. Putnam's indoor exhibits focused on physical anthropology and methodology. He installed an anthropology laboratory where assistants took measurements of visitors and invited them to see how they measured up to statues representing idealized types of Anglo-Saxon manhood and womanhood. The Smithsonian's Bureau of American Ethnology (BAE), on the other hand, built on its success at the 1889 Paris exposition and concentrated on life in the America of 1492. Another BAE exhibit dealt with language and race and emphasized the cultural distinctiveness of Indians, making clear to visitors that racial typologies were legitimate categories for understanding human evolution and that racial types could be arranged into categories of savage and civilized. The BAE exhibit in the Woman's Building also lent legitimacy to

The Dahomeyan Village on the Midway at the World's Columbian Exposition, representing the most "primitive" and "savage" race, was intended to convince white fairgoers of their racial superiority. (Reprinted from *The Cincinnati Post Portfolio of Midway Types* [Chicago: The American Eng. Co. Publishers and Printers, 1893])

popular beliefs about the reality of racial progress through displays of comparative objects of material culture from different cultures.[29]

Though largely unnoticed by the public, the fair management's treatment of African Americans also reinforced the racist thinking of the day. Stung by being overlooked at earlier fairs, black leaders began well before 1893 to demand that the World's Columbian Exposition include exhibits that showed African American achievements, especially since the Civil War. No black representatives sat on the fair's central committee, on any of the state fair commissions, or on the Board of Lady Managers, and so efforts to develop a separate pavilion were fruitless. Fair managers did agree, however, to schedule a special day for black artists and musicians to display their works or to perform their compositions. Some black activists, like Ida B. Wells, a journalist, urged a black boycott of the fair to protest that tokenism, while others, including Frederick Douglass, the revered abolitionist and crusader for black equality, wanted to use the special day for African Americans to show themselves off to their advantage.

What was called Colored People's Day was held on August 25, 1893. Douglass used the occasion to deliver a strong speech denying that there was a "Negro problem" in America. He asserted that the problem lay in the fact that white Americans did not honor their own Constitution in their failure to grant equal rights to African Americans. When Ida Wells heard about the speech, she apologized to Douglass. Together they wrote a pamphlet titled *The Reason Why the Colored American Is Not in the World's Columbian Exposition.* The pamphlet presented evidence of the systematic exclusion of blacks from any responsible role in the fair and condemned fair officials for their immoral and hypocritical attitudes. Unfortunately, whatever impact Douglass and Wells may have had was short lived, as just two years later Booker T. Washington's accommodationist speech at the 1895 Atlanta exposition was much more widely publicized.[30]

The Panic of 1893 did nothing to erode the power of racist thinking. If anything, the economic depression that swept the nation in 1893 led some Americans to conclude that people deemed racially inferior lacked the capacity to determine their own economic and political destinies. With a growing number of economists arguing that foreign markets were necessary to absorb the excess production of U.S. agriculture and industry, the exposition, with its displays of America's surplus production alongside much of the world's perceived backwardness, became a primary vehicle for persuading the general public that U.S. economic expansion overseas was preferable to restructuring the U.S. economy and redistributing wealth along lines suggested by Populist and Socialist reformers.

A case in point was the importance that exposition organizers attached to Latin American markets. That interest was the result of Secretary of State James G. Blaine's encouragement of Pan-Americanism, an attempt to create hemispheric solidarity among the nations of North and South America. Although southern fairs in Atlanta and New Orleans had involved Latin American participation, federal interest had languished until Blaine came to the State Department in 1889 and organized a Pan-American conference in Washington, D.C., in October of that year. In addition he suggested reciprocal trade agreements with Latin American nations and saw the potential of the World's Columbian Exposition to be a showcase for Latin American commerce.

William Curtis, an assistant secretary of state, was charged with integrating Blaine's Pan-Americanism into the exposition. He urged the creation of a Latin American department for the fair that would recruit and coordinate hemispheric participation. The fair board approved the suggestion and allocated $100,000 to Curtis for expenses. Much of that money was spent by a ten-man mission sent to Latin America in 1891 to encourage participation, to seek out exhibits, and to ensure appropriate financial support from national governments. The mission was successful—all the countries agreed to send exhibits to Chicago, and ultimately six nations built their own pavilions, while the others showed their wares in the Agriculture, Horticulture, Mines and Mining, and Woman's Buildings, among others. Curtis also enhanced the Hispanic presence (and the historical theme of the exposition) by arranging for replicas of Columbus's three ships to be sent to Chicago. He also saw to the construction of a replica of La Rábida, the monastery in Spain at which Columbus spent time, and filled it with relics of Columbus's life and voyages. Both the ships and the monastery were among the most popular attractions at the fair.[31]

With a total attendance of more than twenty million and a mountain of favorable publicity, the World's Columbian Exposition was a great aesthetic and cultural success. With a profit of $1.4 million, it was a commercial success as well. When most of the fair was destroyed in 1894 by a fire of mysterious origins, the fair acquired a unique mystique that would perpetuate its memory. More than memories survived the fair, however. Many of the fair's exhibits found their way into museums, especially the Chicago Field Museum, the Philadelphia Commercial Museum, and the Smithsonian Institution. Equally important was the nationalizing ritual that this fair introduced to public schools around the country—the Pledge of Allegiance. Little wonder that this fair became a source of inspiration. As steel magnate Andrew Carnegie put it at the close of the exposition, "the seventeen years that passed between the Philadelphia exhibition and that at Chicago was a period quite long enough." "At least once every twenty years," he insisted, there should be "a national reunion" like the Chicago fair organized in every region of the United States. Carnegie would get his wish several times over as a full-fledged world's fair movement swept the country.[32]

The success of the World's Columbian Exposition became immediately apparent. Many of the exhibits from that fair were shipped to San Francisco and installed at the California Midwinter International Exposition, which

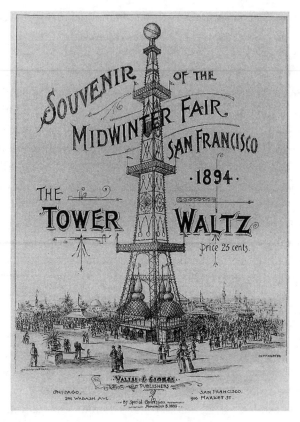

The California Midwinter International Exposition in San Francisco in 1894 marked the first time a world's fair had come to the West Coast. (Photo courtesy of the Larson Collection, Sanoian Special Collections Library, Henry Madden Library, California State University, Fresno)

opened on January 27, 1894. This world's fair, the first to be held on the West Coast, was planned to promote California's mild winter weather to visitors from other parts of the United States. Michel H. de Young, the owner and publisher of the *San Francisco Chronicle,* had been commissioner of the California exhibit at the World's Columbian Exposition and returned to his home state convinced that San Francisco could organize its own exposition. Even before the Chicago fair closed, San Francisco city officials selected a 160-acre site in Golden Gate Park and began construction on fair buildings that were built between August 1893 and January 1894. A

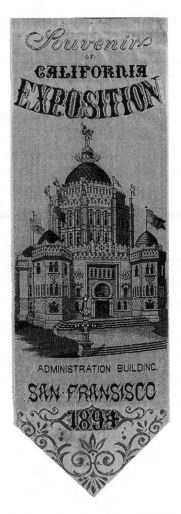

This souvenir ribbon from the California Midwinter International Exposition was popular despite the misspelling of the host city's name. (Photo courtesy of the Larson Collection, Sanoian Special Collections Library, Henry Madden Library, California State University, Fresno)

266-foot-high tower with a searchlight dominated the terraced fairgrounds and the eclectic buildings scattered throughout. Nicknamed the "City of Palms," the Midwinter International Exposition was an intriguing mix of technological and ethnological exhibits in a garden setting. Nearly 1.4 million visitors attended the exposition in its five-month run, and organizers could boast a modest profit. More important, the Midwinter International Exposition proved that a successful fair could be held on the West Coast and inspired the planners of later fairs in Portland, Seattle, San Francisco, and San Diego.[33]

The World's Columbian Exposition, the California Midwinter International Exposition, and the southern fairs in Atlanta and Nashville marked the end of an era in American fair history. The fairs between 1876 and 1897 all shared a number of commonalities. They were organized by the wealthy, white business-oriented elite of their host cities; they showed off the latest in American (and, to a lesser extent, foreign) technological achievement; and they emphasized anthropological exhibits that attempted to persuade the white middle- and upper-class visitors of Anglo-Saxon heritage that they were indeed members of the superior race. Between 1898 and 1916, however, an entirely new dimension appeared in American fairs. Because of the Spanish-American War in 1898, the United States acquired a colonial empire, and fair managers made a major effort, often with the help of the federal government, to display America's new imperial acquisitions, to show how American paternalism was going to benefit the people who had fallen under its domination, and to add another dimension to the ongoing demonstration that Anglo-Saxon racial superiority was an immutable fact of life.

2
FAIRS OF THE IMPERIAL ERA

*I*n April 1898 the United States went to war with Spain. Many Americans were very enthusiastic about this war, particularly because the popular press had been clamoring for American action against Spanish atrocities in Cuba for two years and because the sinking of the American battleship *Maine* two months earlier in Havana's harbor had been blamed on Spanish perfidy. The war was short; it was, as Secretary of State John Hay said, a "splendid little war."[1] At its end the United States was the proud possessor of a colonial empire that included the remote Philippine Islands and Guam, as well as the Caribbean island of Puerto Rico, and a protectorate over Cuba. During the war Hawaii had come under the American flag through annexation. In a more general sense, the Spanish-American War placed the United States among the great powers of the world and forever altered American foreign policy. Never again would the United States fail to be a major presence in global events. That fundamental change in America's place in the world would be clearly manifested in the world's fairs held in the United States between 1898 and 1916, beginning with the Trans-Mississippi and International Exposition, held in Omaha in 1898, and the Pan-American Exposition, held in Buffalo in 1901.

Both of those fairs were more elaborate manifestations of the Chicago fair. The Trans-Mississippi Exposition owed its origins to the favorable firsthand and press reports about the World's Columbian Exposition and a desire on the part of Omaha's commercial organizations to hasten the economic recovery of their region after the 1893 depression and to promote the future progress of the Midwest. Edward Rosewater, a Nebraska state representative and the founder of the *Omaha Bee*, a leading newspaper in the state, handled most of the publicity for the fair, in addition to being one of its principal stockholders. Built on two hundred acres overlooking the Missouri River, the Trans-Mississippi Exposition featured a lagoon and neoclassical buildings painted white (although livened with more color and sculpture than at Chicago), which led to the reuse of the name the "White City." The main entrance, an imposing structure called the Arch of States, displayed the coats of arms of the twenty-three states west of the Mississippi River. Even more impressive than the Arch of States was the exposition's electric lighting. The fair's buildings were outlined with thousands of lightbulbs, which created a spectacular effect for nighttime visitors and impressed French exposition planners, who adopted the idea for the grand 1900 Exposition Universelle in Paris. Most of the technological exhibits related to farm implements and machinery, as might be expected. However, the fair focused primarily on Indians because this fair was the closest geographically to where many Indian tribes lived and because anthropological exhibits had proven popular at earlier fairs.[2]

James Mooney, an Indian specialist with the Smithsonian Institution's Bureau of American Ethnology (BAE), was responsible for most of the Indian exhibits, which he placed in a large mock tepee that served as an anthropological museum. He also devised the Indian Congress, which was modeled after colonial exhibits at recent European fairs in France and Belgium that were meant to show visitors all the benefits of imperialism and territorial conquest. Because the U.S. Congress delayed the appropriation of the $40,000 needed to assemble the Indian Congress, it did not convene until August 4, two months after the fair opened its gates. The congress amounted to a large encampment in which numerous tribes set up housekeeping and through which visitors could wander freely. Intended as a serious lesson in anthropology, the Indian Congress quickly turned into a Wild West show when a group known as the Improved Order of Red Men, a white fraternal organization, persuaded fair managers to stage mock battles between Indians and whites or between different groups of Indians. Mooney was appalled because those battles trivialized the original purpose of the Indian Congress. But they were extremely popular and profitable,

The Grand Court's Venetian lagoon lent Omaha's 1898 Trans-Mississippi and International Exposition an aura of "civilization." Shown here is the U.S. Government Building. (Photo courtesy of John E. Findling)

and a sham battle was made the high point of President William McKinley's visit to the fair in October. The battles, always won by the dominant white race (or, presumably, the more civilized Indian tribe), underscored the message that Indians were a race in decline whose only choices were to submit to white rule or to become extinct.

On the midway at the Trans-Mississippi Exposition, the racism of the fair continued to be apparent with the decision to include an Old Plantation Village that was designed to convince visitors that slavery had been a pleasant experience and a positive good for blacks. The midway also featured a Chinese Village, which was advertised as a chance for visitors to learn about the "sly tricks of the 'heathen Chinee.'" In reality the display included little more than a souvenir shop because the Chinese brought from China for the village disappeared into the menial, largely immigrant labor force. At another attraction, the Streets of Cairo, dancing girls fell afoul of the rule that entertainment should not "descend to the low plane of questionable attractions," and fair managers compelled the dancers to moderate their act. Those managers may have been reacting subtly to the deed of Salvation Army Lt. Dorothy Maurer, who, shortly before Opening Day, was arrested for attempting to destroy statues of nude figures atop the Arch of

States. Fined $75 for her act of vandalism, Maurer said, "It was not for myself but for thousands of young people that I decided to destroy them."[3]

The surprisingly quick victory of the United States in the Spanish-American War and the consequent territorial acquisitions became an unexpected boon to the Trans-Mississippi Exposition. To remind visitors of recent military heroics, there was a large mural painting of the battle of Manila Bay and a multimedia portrayal of the war in Cuba. Late in the run of the fair, Filipino natives were imported to create a Philippine village. Publicity that accompanied the village's opening hinted that some of the natives might be cannibals. Within months U.S. military forces in the Philippines would be combating an insurrection against American imperial rule, and mock Philippine villages would become fixtures in American fairs held before World War I.

The Trans-Mississippi and International Exposition attracted 2.7 million visitors, made money, and was the first in a series of expositions designed, as were European fairs of that era, to demonstrate the desirability of colonialism and its importance to future American peace and prosperity. That theme was first fully played out at the 1901 Pan-American Exposition in Buffalo, New York, and at the 1904 Louisiana Purchase International Exposition in St. Louis.[4]

Organizers of the Pan-American Exposition wanted to display the material progress of the New World during the nineteenth century and to promote better trade relations with Latin America, a theme that had been part of various southern fairs and the World's Columbian Exposition. Another objective was to show off the potential of electric power, using Niagara Falls and its generating capacity. The fair originally had been scheduled for 1899, but the Spanish-American War delayed plans, and then the organizers decided not to compete with the mammoth exposition slated for Paris in 1900.

Although Buffalo seemed an unlikely locale for a fair with a thematic focus on Latin America, exposition organizers played up the importance of transportation connections via the Great Lakes and tried hard to attract the interest and participation of America's neighbors to the south. That task was more difficult than before because the U.S. victory in the Spanish-American War had made some Latin American leaders uneasy about the potentially interventionist tendencies of the United States. Exposition managers tried to flatter Latin Americans by designing the fair buildings in a Spanish

Renaissance style and naming William I. Buchanan, a diplomat and former minister to Argentina, as director general. Still, Latin American participation was somewhat disappointing. Despite Buchanan's efforts, only seven nations built their own pavilions, and most of the other nations sent forgettable exhibits that were housed in various buildings, primarily the Agricultural Building.[5]

A more memorable novelty at the Pan-American Exposition was the organizers' decision to create a colorful decorative scheme for the buildings rather than to replicate yet another "white city." The fair's architects employed a racially encoded hierarchical design: darker, so-called cruder colors at the perimeter gave way to gradually lighter, finer shades in the center of the site. The buildings and exhibits were placed to help coordinate the colors and to be consistent with the clear message that the darker colors represented those people deemed the darker, more primitive races, whereas the lighter colors symbolized those people considered the more advanced, light-skinned races. The visual impact, which was stunning, was made even more so by the looming presence of the signature structure, the 375-foot Electric Tower, which seemed to signify that the pinnacle of civilization was located at the center of the fairgrounds.[6]

From the beginning the exposition's planners selected the Philippine Islands as the centerpiece of the colonial exhibits, although they also envisioned displays from Cuba, Puerto Rico, Alaska, and Hawaii, all part of the effort to justify conquest and the existence of a new colonial empire. By 1901 that justification had become part of the national political debate. William Jennings Bryan, the Democratic candidate for president in 1900, had shaped his campaign around an anti-imperialist theme and had run quite well, given the national excitement following the successful Spanish-American War. With a violent insurrection against American rule under way in the Philippines, many Americans were beginning to wonder if overseas colonial possessions were worth the effort.[7]

To counter the rising tide of anti-imperialism, the U.S. government embraced the Pan-American Exposition. In early 1900 the federal government's exposition board sent Frank E. Hilder, a Spanish-speaking employee of the BAE, to the Philippines to collect artifacts for an anthropological exhibit. Hilder worked hard in the Philippines for a month, acquiring artifacts, taking photographs, and developing statistical tables on the economy. Although he died before the exposition opened, his collection formed the

Shown here is the small but enthusiastic Filipino band in the Philippine Village on the midway at the Pan-American Exposition. (Reprinted from *The Pan American and Its Midway* [Philadelphia: J. Murray Jordan, 1901])

center of the Philippine exhibit and was complemented by additional items obtained from commercial sources and military hardware provided by the War Department.

Exposition planners wanted a Philippine village and even hoped to display the leader of the Philippine insurrection, Emilio Aguinaldo, once he was captured, but the federal government refused to provide any funds for such an attraction. Local exposition authorities went ahead on their own, developed a concession for what they called the Filipino Village, and placed the village on the Pan, Buffalo's midway. In an eleven-acre enclosure, a village that was based on photographs of villages in the Philippines was constructed and populated with a few Filipinos brought over for the occasion. Visitors rode around in carts pulled by water buffalo, leading the *New York Times* to gush, "It is almost as good as a trip to the islands." The village made one point clear: the Filipinos, who were represented as a people indifferent to work, were greatly in need of American intervention and uplift. The Filipino Village was such a successful endeavor that the federal government decided to jump in and began planning for a more elaborate installation at the upcoming St. Louis exposition.

Temple of Music. Buffalo. N.Y. Pan American Exposition Building in which President McKinley was shot September 6th 1901.

The Pan-American Exposition is most often remembered for a tragic historical event: the assassination of President McKinley inside the Temple of Music. (Photo courtesy of John E. Findling)

Many of the other midway attractions were quite popular. The Trip to the Moon and Darkness and Dawn used illusionary techniques to involve the audience in a simulated space journey and a haunted house. Darkest Africa exhibited Africans, and the Infant Incubator exhibited babies. At the Streets of Cairo, the usual dancing girls performed, but some visitors chose to ride camels, causing one observer to comment, "What, by the way, can be the special attraction to the American young woman in being jolted by a camel? On the afternoon when I was there, no fewer than half a dozen girls of eighteen years and upward, generally two on a camel, were bumping through Cairo most ungracefully on those ancient beasts, to the amusement of everybody else."[8]

For all its color and the initial enthusiasm of its planners, the Buffalo fair closed in an atmosphere of gloom and financial disaster. On September 6, while on an official visit to the exposition, President McKinley was shot twice and seriously wounded by Leon Czolgosz, an anarchist. Had McKinley been treated by a doctor other than a gynecologist or had the X-ray machine on display at the fair been used, he might have lived, but he died eight days later of gangrene. The attending physician had failed to find one of the two bullets and had not properly cleaned the wound. After the assassination, some visitors thronged to see the site of the assassination in the Temple of Music, but when the books were closed, fair managers faced a loss of about $3 million. In one important respect the Pan-American Exposition did more to change America than it changed Buffalo. While Buffalo enjoyed very few lasting benefits from the fair, the assassination of McKinley brought the young activist Theodore Roosevelt to the White House. As the century changed, so too did the character of the presidency.[9]

When Theodore Roosevelt gave the keynote address for the dedication of the Louisiana Purchase International Exposition in St. Louis, he did so at the largest, most spectacular fair the country had yet seen. In the early 1890s, St. Louis had competed for the World's Columbian Exposition and had lost out to Chicago, much to the disappointment of St. Louis's civic leaders. At the end of the decade, local luminaries, including former governor David R. Francis, U.S. Representative Richard Bartholdt, and prominent businessman Pierre Chouteau, inaugurated a serious movement to bring a fair to St. Louis that might help to restore an economy hurt by the depression of the mid-1890s and an image badly tarnished by a violent transit workers' strike and revelations of urban political corruption. The upcoming centennial of the Louisiana Purchase in 1903 was noted as an appropriate historical event to celebrate as well.

In early 1901 Francis became president of the newly formed Louisiana Purchase Exposition Company. Fair organizers chose Forest Park as the site for the fair because it was in a respectable part of town and was relatively accessible by public transportation. Much work was done at the park to prepare it for the fair, which grew so large that it spilled over onto the new campus of Washington University, which as yet was unopened to students. Reflecting the influence of the City Beautiful movement that had been inspired by the Chicago exposition, St. Louisans undertook a general campaign of urban improvement, building new streets and new playgrounds and painting old buildings.

The development of the 1,272-acre site (almost twice as large as that of the World's Columbian Exposition) resulted in eight main buildings, neoclassically styled, that fanned out from Festival Hall in the center of the fairgrounds. Foreign pavilions were constructed on Washington University's campus, and its athletic fields and stadium provided venues for the 1904

St. Louis businesses and civic groups played major roles in promoting and supporting the St. Louis 1904 Louisiana Purchase International Exposition. Souvenirs such as this pennant were plentiful. (Photo courtesy of the Larson Collection, Sanoian Special Collections Library, Henry Madden Library, California State University, Fresno)

Olympic Games, which were held in conjunction with the exposition. The midway, known as the Pike, extended to the west from the main entrance for more than 1.5 miles. The Louisiana Purchase Exposition was so large that doctors warned weaker patients to avoid the fair lest they collapse from trying to see it all, and health stations were kept busy treating the fourteen thousand visitors who needed medical attention while touring the fairgrounds.[10]

The usual array of commercial and technological exhibits dominated the main exposition buildings, although David Francis noted, rather grandly, that "so thoroughly does [the fair] represent the world's civilization that if all man's other works were by some unspeakable catastrophe blotted out, the records here established by the assembled nations would afford all necessary standards for the rebuilding of our entire civilization." Goods were arranged in twelve major classifications under the rubric "Man and His Works." Some attention was paid to process as well as product, and visitors could observe diamond cutting, printing, and rope making, among other things. The wide variety of international exhibits also impressed visitors. Sam Hyde, a bookkeeper from Belleville, Illinois, who visited the fair frequently, recalled:

It was somewhat inspiring on entering the grounds to feel that the whole world was there and every nation showing its best products and doing its best to please. Every civilized nation had its sailors, its soldiers and its military band. And there were uniforms as varied and as brilliant as the kaleidoscope. And music to charm the senses or split the ears (according to your taste) at every turn. Perhaps the most popular music was the Filipino military band of sixty pieces. Wonderful tales were told of the extraordinary talent of those little brown fellows.[11]

The Louisiana Purchase International Exposition boasted the most extensive anthropological exhibit of any world's fair. Exposition management asked prominent anthropologists for help in creating a congress of races that would pay particular attention to the most primitive races or ethnic groups. Academic consultants, such as Frederic W. Putnam, who had handled the anthropological exhibits at the World's Columbian Exposition, endorsed the idea, and the directors hired W. J. McGee, a former BAE anthropologist, to head the anthropology department. McGee had a well-defined theory of racial hierarchy based on what he claimed were differences in cranial capacity and manual dexterity among the races. McGee emphasized the white man's burden as the key to worldwide evolutionary human progress.[12]

A believer in living exhibits, McGee created an outdoor laboratory for anthropological fieldwork in the far reaches of the fairgrounds and brought together Pygmies from west Africa, giants from Argentina's Patagonian district, American Indians, and others. Near that enclave was a forty-seven-acre Filipino village, with some twelve hundred natives, which had the full sponsorship of the federal government. Still other ethnological exhibits with a commercial flair attracted fairgoers on the Pike.

An anthropological laboratory, headed by two psychologists from Columbia University, was installed in one of the Washington University buildings used by the exposition. The psychologists carried out all kinds of tests and measurements, including those that purported to link skull size with intelligence, in front of the steady stream of fairgoers visiting the building. They saw the results and left with their belief in Anglo-Saxon racial superiority confirmed by the most up-to-date scientific research methods.[13]

The Filipino village, officially known as the Philippine Reservation, surpassed by far the Filipino presence at the Buffalo fair, partly because of the support of the federal government. William Howard Taft, the governor general of the Philippines, was instrumental in facilitating the exhibit; he thought it would be morally uplifting for the natives and would hasten the completion of pacification on the islands. The federal government created a Philippine Exposition Board to organize the exhibit and appointed William Powell Wilson as its head. Wilson, the director of the Philadelphia Commercial Museum, was well regarded as an exhibit designer. He was assisted by Gustavo Niederlein, a scientist who had made valuable contributions to the French colonial displays at the 1900 Exposition Universelle in Paris.[14]

Visitors to the Philippine Reservation encountered a military museum just inside the main entrance. Beyond that point, they learned, the reservation was divided into three cultural areas representing the Spanish colonial past, the current state of the colony, and the future that might materialize with U.S. tutelage.

The Spanish heritage of the Philippines was represented by a town square with a number of colonial buildings as they might have appeared in Manila during colonial days. The contemporary colonial situation was portrayed by different island tribes in a variety of small villages scattered around the reservation. The most notable (and popular) villages were those of the Negritos, described as "monkey-like," and the Igorots, who caused a stir when they requested dogs to eat, a request that eventually was granted (twenty dogs were brought in from the city pound each week). Another controversy involved the perceived necessity to make the Negritos and Igorots wear more clothes than they usually would. Anthropologists howled in dismay, but the Victorian sensibilities of female visitors were protected.

The third cultural area of the reservation featured the Philippine Scouts and Constabulary, paramilitary units that collaborated with U.S. forces, as examples of what Filipinos could aspire to with American help. The seven hundred Filipinos constituting the scouts and constabulary wore clean, modern uniforms and helped to police the entire reservation.[15]

Along the Pike the most spectacular ethnological exhibits or shows were the Boer War presentation and the Fair Japan concession. In the Boer War exhibit fairgoers could see a mock battle between British and Boer troops, while assorted native South Africans stood around for authenticity. Fair Japan celebrated Japan's recent military success over Russia and also included a display of light-skinned Ainu, aborigines from Japan, who provided many issues for anthropologists to discuss with respect to the place of the Japanese in the racial hierarchy of the world. Sam Hyde was impressed by the Japanese display:

"Of all the foreign nations that participated in the fair, none made so good a showing and won such universal praise as Japan. There must have been many more of the Japs at the fair than were in attendance at their displays for we met them at every turn and never saw one in a bad humor, they were always pleasant when you spoke to them. They are a nation of homely men but the women were fairly goodlooking."

But much of the entertainment along the Pike was much more tawdry, and its appeal to sensuality offended Hyde, who wrote that "if the Pike had been a mile longer it would have led to hell."[16]

For the second time in Olympic history, the summer games were held in conjunction with a world's fair. The games in 1900, conducted within the scope of the Exposition Universelle in Paris, had been an athletic travesty, filled with substandard competitors, bogus events, and limited participation. The St. Louis games of 1904 were hardly better. Many European athletes could not afford the long journey to America to compete, and fair managers, hoping to profit from Olympic publicity, spread the events out over several months and applied the name "Olympic" to virtually every contest of athletic skill held at or near the fairgrounds. The management even linked the Olympics to the fair's anthropological purpose by staging Anthropology Days, two days of athletic games in mid-August. For those games natives were recruited from the various villages and sent to compete in different Olympic events. Because few, if any, of those natives had been training for or were even familiar with the events in which they competed, they did quite poorly compared with the Anglo-Saxon competitors in the actual Olympic Games, and the comparisons were taken as one more sign of the racial superiority of whites. On the second day, people on display as anthropological specimens competed in a number of indigenous sports, and fairgoers marveled at how well or how quickly they performed those customary feats, such as climbing trees. The highlight of the day may have been the Pygmy mud fight, where the native Africans dodged globs of mud thrown at them with incredible agility.[17]

One of the most successful American world's fairs, the Louisiana Purchase International Exposition attracted about twenty million people and earned a considerable profit. It contributed a great deal to the revitalization and prosperity of St. Louis and helped to bring a progressive spirit to the city's political leadership. The exposition also was a major inspiration to individuals and groups on the West Coast who were planning fairs of their own in Portland and Seattle.[18]

Joel M. Long of the Portland Board of Trade initiated discussions about a fair for his city in 1900, and the Oregon Historical Society determined the date and the historical theme—the Lewis and Clark Expedition that had reached Oregon after its exploration of the Louisiana Purchase a hundred years earlier. The success of the 1894 California Midwinter International Exposition and concern about the effects of the depression of the 1890s spurred the thinking of Long and others among the political and cultural elite of Portland; a world's fair might be an excellent way to promote commercial expansion across the Pacific and to assure visitors of the moral correctness of America's imperial design.

The state legislature supported the idea, and fair organizers created an exposition corporation in October 1901. But the progress toward a successful fair did not go smoothly. Opposition to the fair developed within local labor unions in 1902 when fair managers reneged on a promise to employ only union workers on the construction of the fair buildings. That dispute raged for more than two years, while Socialist union leaders demanded a public referendum on the exposition, and union workers feared discrimination when they worked at the site. In 1903, despite the labor problems, Oregon's state legislature appropriated $450,000 for the exposition and appointed a commission to manage the event. A year later the larger and more conservative American Federation of Labor joined with the fair board to settle the labor problem. Fair managers, following the precedents of workers' excursions at earlier fairs, stressed the educational benefits of the fair to workers and promised a special day at the fair for trade unionists. Meanwhile, in 1904 the federal government agreed to participate and ultimately set aside $475,000 for its exhibits, a figure substantially reduced from an original $2 million. Sixteen states other than Oregon participated, and ten built their own pavilions. Not wanting to leave anyone or anything out, fair managers came up with perhaps the most unwieldy formal name in the history of world's fairs: the Lewis and Clark Centennial and American Pacific Exposition and Oriental Fair.[19]

The site for the fair, Guild's Lake, was on the edge of Portland northwest of the center of the city. A pasture and marsh, this area became an industrial district after the fair. The marshes were transformed into a shallow lake at the center of the fairgrounds. Most of the buildings were designed in a Spanish Renaissance style by local architects; the only truly distinctive structure was the Forestry Building, a large log cabin measuring 209 feet by 105 feet, with tree trunks supporting a cathedral-like ceiling.[20]

Given the success of the Filipino exhibits at the St. Louis fair, it was not surprising that the Portland organizers wanted a similar display to highlight their fair. But the War Department, which had subsidized the St. Louis exhibit, was leery about spending too much money (it had overspent its budget for St. Louis) and decided to send only a collection of artifacts. The organizers turned to the private sector and found two amateur anthropologists, Samuel M. McGowan and Truman K. Hunt, and a showman, Edmund A. Felder, who had been involved in the exhibit at St. Louis. Those three men formed the International Anthropological Exhibit Company to stage Filipino exhibits in Portland and all across America, using natives who would be brought over for a two-year period. The company agreed to pay their expenses and to provide some education for them.

In early 1905, however, the International Anthropological Exhibit Company split up, owing to rivalry among the partners; eventually, Felder and a new partner, Richard Schneidewind, received a contract from Portland's fair organizers to provide an Igorot Village. After some further delay waiting for approval from the colonial administration in the Philippines, the village opened on the midway, called the Trail, just six weeks before the Lewis and Clark Exposition closed. Nonetheless, it was very popular, thanks in part to favorable newspaper accounts. Also on the Trail at Portland were Fair Japan, the Streets of Cairo, an Eskimo Village, and the Old Plantation, as well as a vaudeville show featuring black-faced minstrels.

As part of its ongoing effort to allay concerns about agricultural and industrial overproduction, the federal government mounted displays that demonstrated the commercial opportunities that awaited American business overseas. A photographic exhibit showed potential foreign customers—Hispanic or Caribbean Indian families from areas that had fallen under American domination. Other photographs showed Hawaiians, Eskimos, Pacific Islanders, and, of course, Filipinos. As at the fairs in Buffalo and St. Louis, Filipinos were characterized as a racially diverse people, some of whom,

ON THE
TRAIL
1805

ON THE
TRAIL
1905

Humorous postcards such as this one created for the Portland 1905 Lewis and Clark Centennial and American Pacific Exposition and Oriental Fair were popular with fairgoers, and those receiving the cards enjoyed them too. (Photo courtesy of John E. Findling)

such as Negritos and Igorots, had not progressed very far up the path of civilization and were represented as being on the verge of extinction.[21]

Most of the American exhibits related to regional natural resources, including forestry and fishing. Efforts to obtain foreign exhibits from Asia were hampered by reports of discrimination that some Asians had experienced at the fair in St. Louis. The management did receive some Japanese exhibits sent over to be shown in the Oriental Exhibits Building, the interior of which was purposefully painted red, white, and blue and entirely draped with matching bunting.

The Lewis and Clark Exposition attracted 2.6 million visitors. Most came from the Pacific Northwest; relatively few people made the long journey from east of the Rocky Mountains. Nevertheless, the fair earned a profit of nearly $85,000, launched an annual Rose Festival, and made a few Portlanders richer by bringing in new investment and sparking a real estate boom, outcomes happily emphasized by promoters of subsequent fairs on the West Coast.[22]

Shortly after the close of the Lewis and Clark Exposition, planning began for Seattle's first world's fair, the Alaska-Yukon-Pacific Exposition. Spear-

Commercial and industrial growth of the Pacific Northwest was the motivation behind the Alaska-Yukon-Pacific Exposition. (Photo courtesy of the Larson Collection, Sanoian Special Collections Library, Henry Madden Library, California State University, Fresno)

headed by a banker, John E. Chilberg, and a number of other business and community leaders, many of whom were members of the Alaska Club, an offshoot of the Chamber of Commerce, those discussions centered around holding a fair to extol the virtues of Alaska and its resources. Further thinking led to the addition of Pacific commerce as a related theme. Most of the financial backing came from local railroads, banks, and newspapers. As in Portland, opposition to the Seattle fair developed within the labor community over the issue of the open shop. Labor leaders, mainly Socialists, condemned the exposition and feared that its long-term effect on organized labor would be detrimental.

Fair organizers chose a 250-acre site near the campus of the University of Washington, and the Olmsted Brothers, a landscape architecture firm from Boston, laid out the site design. John Langley Howard, the architect of the University of California at Berkeley, designed the exposition buildings in a standard neoclassical style, although the Forestry Building, like the one at Portland, used tree trunks in its design and construction. To save money, the fair managers included fewer sculptures and fountains than had been the case at most earlier fairs. The midway at the fair, known as the Pay

COLLONADES OF THE
FORESTRY BUILDING,
ALASKA-YUKON
PACIFIC EXPOSITION,
SEATTLE, WASH. 1909.
OFFICIAL POST CARD

The Forestry Building at the Seattle 1909 Alaska-Yukon-
Pacific Exposition, with tree trunks serving as columns, was
unique compared with the other structures on the fair site.
(Photo courtesy of John E. Findling)

Streak, was built in "Japanese-Alaskan" style and featured Japanese
lanterns, Native Alaskan totem poles, and the usual assortment of entertainment attractions, including Roltair's Original House Upside Down,
which amused visitors with its clever placement of angled mirrors that created optical illusions and challenged one's sense of spatial relationships.[23]

At the A-Y-P, as the fair was popularly known, officials invited Alfred C.
Haddon, an anthropologist from Cambridge University, to consult about
racial exhibits and to teach a course on race and culture during the fair, using the native villages and other exhibits as part of his course. As had be-

Roltair's Original House Upside Down was a popular attraction on the Alaska-Yukon-Pacific's Pay Streak. (Photo courtesy of the Larson Collection, Sanoian Special Collections Library, Henry Madden Library, California State University, Fresno)

come standard by that time, an Igorot Village was prominently placed on the Pay Streak, where it became a favorite tour stop for school children who came to the site even before the fair opened. Another anthropological exhibit along the Pay Streak was an Eskimo Village, which included native Siberians and other ethnic Alaskans; the message that was communicated suggested that racial characteristics were a primary indicator of progress.

Government exhibits buttressed some of the Pay Streak concessions. Displays from the federal government occupied one large building and three smaller adjunct buildings, one each for exhibits from Alaska, Hawaii, and the Philippines. Those buildings were filled with static displays prepared by the Smithsonian Institution. Of those, the Filipino building was the most popular, attracting five thousand visitors a day, who learned, in theory, that the American occupation of the Philippines was necessary for the uplifting of the Filipinos and for the commercial benefit of the United States.[24]

Although Seattle was distant from much of the United States, the A-Y-P still boasted a paid attendance of 2.8 million people (a total of 3.7 million attended) and a modest profit of $63,676. It left several buildings to the University of Washington campus and a memorable legacy that contributed to Seattle's decision to hold another world's fair in 1962.[25]

Igorot and Eskimo children from the many villages on display at the Alaska-Yukon-Pacific Exposition. (Photo courtesy of the Larson Collection, Sanoian Special Collections Library, Henry Madden Library, California State University, Fresno)

The Panama-Pacific International Exposition (PPIE) in San Francisco in 1915 was the largest American fair between the Louisiana Purchase International Exposition in 1904 and the fairs in Chicago and New York in the 1930s. The St. Louis fair of 1904 and the beginning of construction of the Panama Canal prompted discussion among San Francisco businessmen who thought that such a fair in their city would be a good way to promote the city's commercial opportunities to the rest of the country. The catastrophic earthquake and fire of 1906 created a greater determination to stage an exposition that would celebrate the city's recovery from that tragedy, and it seemed logical to coordinate the timing of the fair with the completion of the canal.

It was not until February 1911 that the federal government voted its support for San Francisco and the Panama-Pacific International Exposition. Both New Orleans and San Diego had also sought federal sanction for fairs to celebrate the completion of the Panama Canal, and the Louisiana city had a strong claim by virtue of being the closest American port to the canal. San Francisco's boosters reached accommodation with fair organizers in San Diego, however, by agreeing to support that city's bid for a smaller re-

Get your Congressmen
TO VOTE FOR THE
PANAMA-PACIFIC
INTERNATIONAL EXPOSITION
AT THE EXPOSITION CITY
SAN FRANCISCO-1915
CALIFORNIA GUARANTEES AN EXPOSITION
THAT WILL BE A CREDIT
TO THE NATION.

Competition for the 1915 Panama-Pacific International Exposition and lobbying for congressional support for San Francisco are depicted in this world's fair promotional card. (Photo courtesy of the Larson Collection, Sanoian Special Collections, Henry Madden Library, California State University, Fresno)

gional exposition. Then, helped by a massive postcard campaign, San Francisco beat out New Orleans in the battle before Congress.

Although some wanted to place the fair in Golden Gate Park, where the 1894 California Midwinter International Exposition had taken place, the fair's organizers finally decided to use an undeveloped parcel of land on the bay next to the Presidio military installation. The site was laid out in a series of plazas, or courtyards, rather than along wide avenues as in past expositions, and each of the principal plazas was developed by a different architect and surrounded by exhibition buildings, which also served to block chilly breezes from the bay. The style of the exhibition buildings was generally neoclassical, but each principal structure had a dome, giving rise to the nickname "City of Domes." Of those domes the most spectacular was the huge glass dome of the Palace of Horticulture, which was larger than the dome of St. Paul's Cathedral in London. Near the center of the fairgrounds stood the 432-foot-high Tower of Jewels, which was laden with allegorical figures and draped with more than one hundred thousand pieces of colored cut glass linked to tiny mirrors. An elaborate system of indirect lighting made the glass look like precious jewels. The fair buildings, which were constructed out of an artificial travertine substance developed by the architectural firm of McKim, Mead, and White, were tinted in a palette of pastel shades, and under the direction of John McLaren, a park designer, hundreds of trees and shrubs were transplanted on the site.[26]

The PPIE was more concerned with fine art than many previous fairs had been. A. Stirling Calder, who had served on the St. Louis fair's fine arts advisory committee, organized a large assortment of outdoor sculptures, and the Palace of Fine Arts (the only surviving structure from the fair) was filled with more than 11,400 paintings, drawings, and other artworks from all over the world created within the previous ten years. The fair organizers also scheduled a full program of concerts, with guest appearances by some of the most revered names in classical music. For those not so inclined to serious music, John Philip Sousa's band played concerts almost daily.

Technological displays focused on the automobile, which had been growing in popularity and affordability ever since it had been a principal exhibit for the first time at the St. Louis fair. The PPIE included a Ford assembly line that produced eighteen autos every day. Aviation (then called "aeronautics") was also a popular attraction at the fair, and the dangers inherent in its early days were dramatized before a crowd of 50,000 when Lincoln Beachy, perhaps the most famous stunt flyer in America, was killed on March 14, 1915, when his plane broke apart as he tried to come out of a free fall at 3,000 feet. The fair also displayed a transcontinental telephone line, marking the beginning of long distance telephone service, various aviation demonstrations, color photography, and a working Underwood typewriter that was fifteen feet high and weighed fourteen tons.[27]

Fair managers decided not to have a separate anthropology department with extensive exhibits of live subjects. Rather, they resorted to making their anthropological point by means of static exhibits and midway concessions, leaving the more extensive exhibits and demonstrations to the San Diego exposition. As an alternative, and as a service to the public, the PPIE included race-related topics among a long series of scholarly meetings on various contemporary issues that were held during the fair. Some 948 "congresses" were held, several of which touched on the theme of "race betterment," or what eugenics was all about in those days. Much of the inspiration for those race-related meetings came from John H. Kellogg, a cereal magnate and head of the Race Betterment Foundation, who suggested that a national registry be created to enable people to avoid pairings with the

Whimsical exhibits such as this knight and horse made of prunes were typical of world's fairs, and fairgoers appreciated them just as much as the industrial, mechanical, and technological displays. (Photo courtesy of the Larson Collection, Sanoian Special Collections Library, Henry Madden Library, California State University, Fresno)

"racially unfit." Others argued for preventing "improper intermarriages" and for promoting selective breeding, suggesting that it was no longer necessary to demonstrate which race was superior. The task was to find ways in which to make that superior race even better. In the Palace of Education, a race betterment booth displayed statues of classical gods to show off the best in human form; to help visitors get the message, other exhibits showed how selective breeding had improved animal stock. In addition a U.S. Department of Labor exhibit presented statistics and a film about immigrants that hinted strongly that the large numbers of immigrants crowding America's shores were weakening the racial purity of Anglo-Saxon Americans.[28]

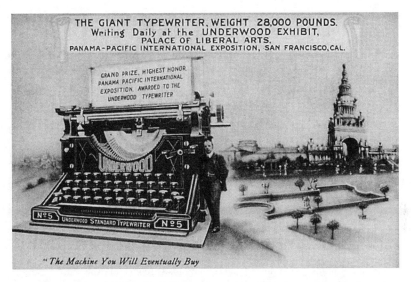

THE GIANT TYPEWRITER, WEIGHT 28,000 POUNDS.
Writing Daily at the UNDERWOOD EXHIBIT,
PALACE OF LIBERAL ARTS,
PANAMA-PACIFIC INTERNATIONAL EXPOSITION, SAN FRANCISCO,CAL.

GRAND PRIZE, HIGHEST HONOR
PANAMA PACIFIC INTERNATIONAL
EXPOSITION, AWARDED TO THE
UNDERWOOD TYPEWRITER

UNDERWOOD

N°5 UNDERWOOD STANDARD TYPEWRITER N°5

"*The Machine You Will Eventually Buy*

The Underwood typewriter on display at the Panama-Pacific International
Exposition left quite an impression on fairgoers. (Photo courtesy of the Larson
Collection, Sanoian Special Collections Library, Henry Madden Library,
California State University, Fresno)

In the garishly lit Joy Zone, the PPIE midway, the high point for visitors
was a working scale model of the Panama Canal, complete with a description that fairgoers could hear on telephone receivers as they glided around
the five-acre exhibit on moving sidewalks. Visitors drawn to exoticism could
see replicas of a Mexican village, a Samoan village, and an African village,
as well as the Mysterious Orient, Japan-Beautiful, and a Chinese village,
which portrayed China as a land ripe for American investment.

The Joy Zone also continued another trend that began on the Midway
Plaisance at the 1893 World's Columbian Exposition in Chicago: the com-
mercialization and commodification of sex. At the Chicago fair several
midway concessions had featured the *danse du ventre*—so called because
the phrase "belly dance" was deemed too vulgar for Victorian sensibilities.
Drawing mixed but overwhelmingly male audiences, those shows had
proven financially successful and inspired the creation of similar attractions
at subsequent fairs, often in "oriental" villages depicting people from the
Middle East. On the Joy Zone in San Francisco, the *danse* took on a novel
form in a larger-than-life painting called *Stella* complete with a mechani-
cally driven rotating belly.[29]

A group of friends and family are packed and ready to go and experience adventure and excitement at the 1915 Panama-Pacific International Exposition. (Photo courtesy of the Larson Collection, Sanoian Special Collections Library, Henry Madden Library, California State University, Fresno)

By the time the PPIE closed in December 1915, nearly nineteen million visitors had passed through its gates, dispelling the fears of promoters who thought that the outbreak of war in Europe would have a dampening effect on attendance. The exposition was financially successful as well, allowing fair directors to pay off their mortgage in August and wind up with a profit of more than $2.4 million. Many of the exhibits were shipped down the coast to San Diego, where the Panama California Exposition was gearing up for its second season.[30]

San Diego's exposition, which had been relegated to regional status after losing its competition with the San Francisco fair to be the primary celebrant of the completion of the Panama Canal, was situated in four hundred acres of the fourteen hundred acre Balboa Park, formerly known as City Park. The landscape architecture firm of the Olmsted Brothers wanted the site to lie on the edge of the park to preserve as much natural beauty as possible, but local politicians insisted on a central site, facilitating the construction of a tramline that would later be extended to the northern suburbs. The Olmsteds were so unhappy with that decision that they withdrew from the project.

One of the main features of the San Diego fair was its clear attempt to reinvent history to help build an urban identity for the city. Much of southern California's population had arrived within a generation of the fair, and the city still had a midwestern air, especially in its dour Republican politics and imitative Victorian architecture. Exposition planners were more comfortable with the city's politics than its architecture. To change the course of the city's architecture, and therefore its identity, they hit upon this scheme: throughout the fair they would create a romanticized vision of the city's Spanish heritage, transforming the fair into a Spanish/Mediterranean colonial city—a West Coast "city on a hill" that would rival what the Puritans had tried to accomplish in New England three centuries earlier.[31]

Although the planners originally hoped to build the fair in a simple Spanish mission style, the principal architect, Bertram Goodhue, lobbied successfully for replacing the mission architecture with a much more elaborate baroque Spanish-Mexican colonial style, with the main buildings laid out along a single street called the Prado. In addition to the numerous buildings (many of which still stand because of the city's commitment to historic preservation and its warm, dry climate), the site was landscaped to create an abundant Mediterranean atmosphere.[32]

While the Panama California Exposition had its share of technological exhibits and demonstrations, the promoters decided to emphasize what they termed the science of man, or anthropology, at their fair. In 1911 exposition officials appointed Edgar L. Hewett, the director of the American Institute of Archeology in Santa Fe, to develop exhibits on the evolutionary progress of humans. The fair's directors pledged that the exhibits would be housed in a permanent museum in San Diego after the fair closed, and they lived up to their promise, creating the Museum of Man in Balboa Park.

Hewett consulted closely with William Henry Holmes and Aleš Hrdlička of the Smithsonian Institution; Holmes agreed to mount an exhibit of stone art for the fair, and Hrdlička became head of the division of physical anthropology at the fair. The anthropologists worked out plans for a three-part presentation that would include separate exhibits on the physical evolution of man, the evolution of culture, and the native races of America. Hrdlička and other anthropologists traveled around Europe and Asia in search of skeletal evidence of distinctive racial types for the exhibit, while others went to Africa, Alaska, and ancient Indian sites in the Americas for other pieces of the evolutionary puzzle.

This publicity label for the Panama California Exposition
of 1915 in San Diego suggests the distinctive architecture of
that fair. (Photo courtesy of John E. Findling)

When all the exhibit material had been collected, it was displayed in
three of the exhibit buildings in such a way that visitors could easily conclude that human beings could be divided into distinctive racial categories.
One exhibit showed differences among historic races by reconstructed
skulls and other skeletal features. Another compared specimens of different
races throughout their life spans. A third compared present-day races, dividing them into white, yellow-brown, and black groups, which then were
subdivided into a number of secondary races. Hrdlička also sought to project anthropology into the future with an exhibit that suggested how anthropologists might be able to regulate racial evolution in years to come,
thus linking the anthropology exhibits in San Diego with the eugenics exhibits in San Francisco.[33]

On the Isthmus, San Diego's midway, the usual panorama of live,
racially charged shows and villages prevailed. The Japanese Streets of Joy,
Chinatown, and the Painted Desert all reinforced the racial stereotypes portrayed in the anthropology exhibits. For example, the Painted Desert,

International Panama-California Exposition, San Diego, California.
Out-door Oven in The Painted Desert.

This scene from the Painted Desert concession at the Panama California Exposition no doubt made visitors appreciate their gas stoves back home. (Photo courtesy of John E. Findling)

which was financed by the Atchison, Topeka, and Santa Fe Railroad, was a Pueblo Indian village, showing Indians living a simple hand-to-mouth existence. Directly across the street was International Harvester's Model Farm, a mechanized farm that suggested that Anglo-Saxon technology was the key to human success.[34]

The Panama California Exposition was successful enough that its managers kept it open for a second season in 1916. It accomplished its aim of reinventing a history for San Diego and left enough goodwill that San Diegans organized another fair just twenty years later. Less than six months after the final closing of the Panama California Exposition, however, the United States found itself embroiled in a war that would bring massive and unforeseen economic, political, and social changes to the world. The next generation of fairs, those held between the two world wars, would reflect many of those changes in their organization, content, and legacies.

3
FAIRS BETWEEN
THE WORLD WARS

*I*n the United States the end of World War I and the failure of the Senate to ratify the Treaty of Versailles put a disillusioned American public in a foul mood about internationalism. The 1920s was a decade of prosperity for many Americans, which contributed to a heightened sense of consumerism and a lack of concern for overseas problems. Although some American businesses were making money from foreign investments or trade, most middle-class Americans in the 1920s indulged in the pleasures of consumption, enjoying jazz music, bootlegged alcohol, and fast cars. To be sure, that behavior was not universally shared in the United States during the decade. For many farmers, African Americans, and working-class Americans, who lived at or below the poverty line, the 1920s were a cruel and bitter time. No aid was forthcoming from the conservative federal government, and private charities could help only a small minority of the disadvantaged.

But for those who were caught up in the fervor of the Roaring Twenties and were benefiting from the decade's prosperity, it seemed like a good time to throw a party. The organizers of Philadelphia's Sesqui-Centennial International Exposition in 1926 agreed and seized on the 150th anniversary of American independence as the occasion for a celebration. They were also inspired by the revival of world's fairs in Europe after the war. That revival had been kicked off with the 1924–25 Wembley British Empire Exhibition and the 1925 Paris Exposition Internationale des Arts Décoratifs et Industriales Modernes. Held on the outskirts of London, the Empire Exhibition celebrated British imperial expansion around the globe and attracted twenty-seven million visitors over a two-season run. The Paris fair took as its theme modernistic designs and celebrated the dramatic new art and architectural style that came to be known as art deco.

Promoters of the Sesqui-Centennial Exposition eschewed both overseas imperialism and modern art and focused instead on overt historical themes drawn from the American Revolution. The idea for the fair originated in 1916 with department store magnate John Wanamaker, who had been a member of the finance committee for the 1876 Centennial International Exhibition. Because of World War I, however, no serious planning took place until 1920, when Mayor J. Hampton Moore invited civic leaders to a meeting on November 4. At that meeting the idea of a fair was endorsed, and the mayor appointed a Committee of One Hundred to carry out some preliminary planning. Although President Warren G. Harding endorsed the idea, the United States Congress refused the planning committee's request for a $20 million subsidy but eventually provided $2 million for the construction of its own pavilion and exhibits. The Pennsylvania state government was no more generous, and so most of the funding for the exposition came from the city government.

Although the fair planners considered using the old Centennial Exhibition site in Fairmount Park for the Sesqui-Centennial Exposition, they selected a tract of city-owned land in south Philadelphia near the League Avenue navy yard. That land, however, was quite swampy and required huge amounts of fill as well as special foundations for the buildings, which added to both the time for construction and the cost of the fair. Preparations lagged so far behind schedule in 1925 that David Collier, the director general (and the former president of the Panama California Exposition in San Diego), resigned. A new management team, headed by Capt. Asher C. Baker, who had worked with fairs in Paris (1900), St. Louis (1904), and San Francisco (1915), scaled back the original plans, reduced from five to three the number of principal exhibition buildings, and laid off 26 of the 120 fair employees. There was talk among exposition planners of delaying the opening of the fair until later in 1926, or even until the following year, but Mayor W. Freeland Kendrick, who had become the prime crusader for the fair, insisted on the May 31 opening date, so that it would coincide with the national Shriners' convention scheduled to be held in Philadelphia. As a result many of the buildings were not finished by the time the fair opened.[1]

This commemorative stamp issued for Philadelphia's Sesqui-Centennial International Exposition of 1926 portrays the historical emphasis of the fair. (Photo courtesy of John E. Findling)

Rain dampened the opening ceremonies and kept crowds down, despite the promise of speeches by Secretary of State Frank Kellogg and Secretary of Commerce Herbert Hoover. Another speaker at the opening ceremonies was A. Philip Randolph, the African American head of the Brotherhood of Railroad Sleeping Car Porters, the most important African American union. Randolph was added at the last minute after a delegation of "representative colored citizens" had demanded that an African American be part of the ceremonies. Exposition officials probably had in mind a speech similar to the one that Booker T. Washington had delivered at the Atlanta fair in 1895. But they were caught off guard. Randolph's speech, a plea for social justice for black Americans, was the longest of any of the speeches in the program, but it received little notice in the white press outside of Philadelphia and was never mentioned in the fair's official history.[2]

Visitors on opening day, including the Shriners, were disappointed because the fair was only about 75 percent completed and would not be totally finished for another month. Many of the Shriners and other visitors went home after their convention and told their friends and neighbors that the exposition was a fraud, an opinion shared by many local residents. A visitor from Iowa, James McHenry, summed up the impressions of many early fairgoers:

This thing reminds me of a guy I knew in Ioway [*sic*]. He invited a raft of friends and relatives to a big birthday dinner and surprise party one time. He got so darned excited about how many he was going to have, invitations, his speech of welcome, and the program of entertainment, he plumb forgot to order any grub. When he thought of it, everybody was there, the stores closed, and he in a heck of a fix! But the fellow had a good sense of humor. Come around next birthday and we'll have something to eat, said he. Maybe I will.[3]

It was a further bad omen that Director General Baker died on June 5, leaving a void in the exposition's leadership.

Probably the most significant structure of the Sesqui-Centennial Exposition was a one hundred thousand–seat stadium that hosted the opening ceremonies and a variety of other events, including the extravagant heavyweight championship fight between Jack Dempsey and Gene Tunney. That fight occurred in the wake of controversy as well. In March Mayor Kendrick had refused permission to use the stadium for a heavyweight championship bout between Dempsey and challenger Harry Wills, stating that such a match "would detract from the primary purpose for which the mammoth stadium was constructed—a program of events arranged purely for . . . the visitors [to] the Ses-Qui." Although the mayor failed to mention that Wills was African American, that fact was not lost on the black community, and the hypocrisy of Kendrick's statement was a matter of widespread comment when he approved the Dempsey-Tunney match a few months later. African Americans were also outraged when they learned that the national Ku Klux Klan had reserved the auditorium for a special program between September 9 and 11. After a good deal of controversy, fair officials revoked the Klan's permit in July, citing the possible threat to public safety that the presence of large numbers of Klansmen would represent.[4]

More than most other fairs, the Sesqui-Centennial Exposition stuck to a historical focus. One of the most spectacular sights was the eighty-foot-tall model of the Liberty Bell outlined in twenty-six thousand electric lights. While the major exhibit buildings displayed a historically neutral architectural style, many smaller structures were built in an eighteenth-century colonial revival style, including replicas of noteworthy historic buildings such as New York City's Federal Hall and Virginia's Mount Vernon. A good deal of colonial architecture was concentrated in High Street, a replica of colonial Philadelphia's Market Street, with twenty houses containing exhibits, restaurants, shops, and organizational headquarters. High Street was largely the work of the Sesqui-Centennial Exposition's Women's Department, whose members planned the exhibits in the various houses and served as guides in period costumes. Most of the exhibits pertained to colonial history, although the League of Women Voters sponsored a display that highlighted the newly won right of women to vote. The popularity of High Street contributed to the development of outdoor historical museums and villages around the country, one of the major legacies of this exposition.[5]

Although the Sesqui-Centennial Exposition did not emphasize science and technology, it did introduce a number of new features into fair history. Those items included radio advertisements, talking motion pictures, and electrically amplified public address systems, which reflected the technological advances that marked the 1920s in the United States.[6]

By early October, nearly two months before the closing date, it was clear that the exposition was going to be a financial failure. On October 7 Mayor Kendrick announced that the total attendance would fall short of five million, far below the twenty-eight to thirty-five million that some had forecast, and that the city would have to make up the deficit. There were rumors about graft and press accounts of mismanagement, but the real culprits were poor planning and some unusually bad weather. Although serious planning had begun in 1920, it had not progressed evenly and coherently, and many decisions were postponed until it was too late to implement them carefully. The opening of the fair should have been delayed, but Kendrick, a Shriner, had insisted that the fair open during the national Shriners' convention. The weather, too, was a major factor. It rained 86 of the 130 days the fair was open and washed out 18 of a scheduled 29 performances of the extravagant pageant, *Freedom*, which organizers had hoped would be a major drawing card for the exposition.

When the Sesqui-Centennial International Exposition finally closed on November 30, it left behind a $5 million deficit, although many felt that its patriotic purposes had been successfully accomplished. The fair cost Philadelphia a total of $17 million, plus another $3 million in certificates sold to local residents who would not be able to redeem them as had been hoped. Total attendance had climbed to over 6.4 million, although far fewer paid the full fifty cent admission price.[7]

While the Sesqui-Centennial International Exposition was taking place, the city of Long Beach, California, was putting the finishing touches on some extensive improvements to its harbor facilities. To publicize the harbor improvements and to promote trade, civic leaders decided to stage a small world's fair, the 1928 Pacific Southwest Exposition. It was held on sixty-three acres near the harbor, so that the fairgrounds were accessible by both automobile and boat. The fair board elected to globalize its regional focus and to center the fair's theme on Tunisia, a North African country whose climate and trade-dominated economy resembled those of Long Beach.

Fair buildings were low, white, stuccoed structures, with flat roofs punctuated by domes and towers. Like a large movie set, the fair, steeped in the exoticism of earlier representations of northern Africa in previous American expositions, was built quickly and was designed to be demolished after the closing ceremonies. Exhibits in the various buildings consisted principally of goods and cultural artifacts from Europe, Asia, and the countries of the west coast of South America, where, American businessmen hoped, significant trade relations would develop. A midway, called the Amusement Zone, featured the usual entertainment attractions, while an impressive pageant celebrated the history of the American Southwest.

A total of 1.1 million people attended the Pacific Southwest Exposition, which closed on September 3, 1928, after just a six-week run. On that final day the tower atop the Palace of Fine Arts collapsed, injuring a woman. The accident was attributed to poor construction. Just over a year later, the stock market — perhaps another victim of poor construction — collapsed also.[8]

When the stock market took its initial plunge in October 1929, planning for the first great American world's fair of the 1930s had been under way for nearly two years. Chicago was to celebrate its centennial in 1933, and ten years before the idea to mark that occasion with a world's fair had first surfaced. After some political infighting in the mid-1920s, a board of directors was created in late 1927, with oil tycoon and banker Rufus Dawes as its chairman. Dawes was well connected; his brother, Charles G. Dawes, was Calvin Coolidge's vice president from 1925 to 1929. Dawes and the board chose Lenox Lohr, a retired military officer and engineer, as general manager of the fair.

Early in its planning the fair board decided to focus on progress through science as the major theme of the fair, knowing that a strictly historical theme, such as Philadelphia had tried, would not be widely attractive. That notion led to the name of the fair — A Century of Progress — that the board formally chose in June 1929 to replace the awkward, self-deprecating "Chicago's Second World's Fair," which had been the working name of the fair until 1929. It was clear to everyone that science had made tremendous strides in the hundred years since the founding of Chicago in 1833. To assist with the development of science exhibits, exposition planners enlisted the support of the National Research Council, an organization of scientists that had been formed in 1916 to advise on wartime matters and had never been disbanded.

Reflecting their conservative Republican economic beliefs, the fair board chose not to seek direct government subsidization for the Century of Progress. They raised money privately instead by selling memberships in the Chicago World's Fair Legion, which raised $634,000 and generated a great deal of free publicity. The board also offered a $10 million public bond issue, of which $6.1 million was actually paid in, and raised an additional $3 million in concessionaires' contracts. The federal government spent $1 million on its own pavilion and exhibits.[9]

Unlike the planners of the World's Columbian Exposition forty years earlier, the fair's board of directors engaged in little debate over the choice of a site. The board chose a site just south of downtown Chicago, on a long, narrow strip of land that bordered Lake Michigan for about three miles. At no point was the site wider than one-quarter of a mile, and the northern end was divided by a sizable lagoon, all of which made it difficult for architects to develop a coherent site plan. The fair board appointed an architectural commission to lay out the site and to design the buildings. Not surprisingly, that design resembled what had been done in 1893 because the secretary of the architectural commission was Daniel H. Burnham Jr., son of the Chicago architect who had assembled the commission and supervised the construction for the World's Columbian Exposition.

One of the first decisions the architects made was to create fair buildings that reflected the theme of scientific progress. For that reason (and because nobody wanted to imitate the earlier fair), the commission rejected the neoclassical architecture that had proven so popular at previous fairs. Modernism had been successfully implemented at fairs in Paris in 1925, in Barcelona and Seville in 1929, and again in Paris in 1931, which significantly influenced the architects of the Century of Progress Exposition.

Although architectural planning began before the onset of the Great Depression, that financial crisis forced the fair management and the architects to scale down their building plans. As a consequence, the fair's architecture and buildings became models of great economy. The simple designs of

The logo of Chicago's Century of Progress Exposition in 1933–34 illustrates the modernistic style of this fair and was found on many souvenirs such as this compact. (Photo courtesy of John E. Findling)

most of the buildings employed flat windowless walls, inexpensive building materials, and virtually no exterior ornamentation. Color and light were used to provide aesthetic beauty, and the fair board hired noted stage set designer Joseph Urban to devise a color scheme.[10]

By 1933 the use of bright colors in consumer products and popular entertainment, such as clothing, home appliances, automobiles, advertisements, and films, had become common. Color as an essential ingredient of modernism in art and design dated at least from the 1925 Paris Exposition Internationale des Arts Décoratifs et Industriels Modernes. Urban had spent fifteen years as set designer for the New York Metropolitan Opera, where he had made good use of both color and lighting. At the Century of Progress, he employed color to unify buildings designed by different architects and to connect them with nearby structures. Urban's plan involved a total of twenty-three colors, although only three or four were used on each building. Black, white, blue, and orange were the predominant colors, but many others were used for detail work or special effects. The colors were indeed bright and bold, but they did not please everyone. Critic Douglas Haskell, writing in the *Architectural Review,* thought that the effect was more "curious than beautiful," and the health columnist of the *Chicago Tribune* advised readers to wear dark glasses when visiting the fair so as not to fall victim to "severe eye strain, [which] causes a sort of pus formation."[11]

Westinghouse and General Electric designed the lighting for most of the fair and made good use of indirect and colored lighting. The distant inspiration for dramatic lighting effects came from the 1901 Pan-American Exposition in Buffalo; the more immediate inspiration came from the Barcelona and Seville expositions of 1929, where colored lighting was used effectively on buildings and in fountains. Streets and walkways were draped with other colored lights, some designed in the form of "lotus-like glass fountains that shimmered in the long delicate tendrils like water jets in a fountain." The lighting designers at the Century of Progress surpassed the Spanish fairs by using gaseous tube lighting for the first time at a world's fair. In most cases the tube lighting was seen only as a reflected light, but on an exterior wall of the Electrical Building, nearly a mile of green and blue tube lighting resembled a fifty-five-foot-high waterfall. That particular feature was done as an economy measure over the protests of building architect Raymond Hood, who wanted to construct a real waterfall. Another significant lighting feature was a bank of twenty-four arc searchlights located at the southern end of the fairgrounds. At night those searchlights fanned the sky and occasionally intersected with another bank of searchlights located near the northern end of the site.[12]

The most notable structures at the Century of Progress were the 628-foot-tall twin towers that supported the Sky Ride, a cable car that traversed the fairgrounds, taking visitors across the lagoon at the northern end. Among the exhibit buildings, the most distinctive was the Travel and Transport Building, part of which was a 125-foot-tall round structure with a fluted exterior that featured a domelike roof suspended by an elaborate cable system that left the interior space free of columns or other support members. The roof's suspension system was also fitted with expansion joints that allowed it to move up to eighteen inches depending on weather conditions. Although the Travel and Transport Building was a remarkable piece of engineering

The Travel and Transport Building at the Century of Progress Exposition represented a form of futuristic architecture that never became a part of mainstream design. (Photo by Peter M. Warner, reprinted with permission from Charles Warner)

design, it did not please the critics and did not become a model for future buildings of its purpose. On the whole, however, the architecture of the Century of Progress can be seen as transitional: it led the way into the era of modernism, further popularized an architecture based on art deco design principles and the international style, and the streamlined style in industrial design. Five years later this architecture would reach a fuller flowering at the New York World's Fair, a fair in which America's most noted industrial designers played a prominent role.[13]

Wherever possible, exhibits at the Century of Progress tried to demonstrate the process of making something rather than the finished product. Such a focus, it was reasoned, would create more dynamic exhibits and would be more interesting to visitors. The fair board decided to coordinate the pure science exhibits itself and to rely on private corporations to show examples of applied science. To do its part, the board enlisted a group of distinguished scientists in different fields who developed exhibits in biology, chemistry, physics, geology, mathematics, and medicine. Most of those exhibits were placed in the Hall of Science, the largest and most important exhibit building of the fair. Most of the applied science exhibits were located in corporate pavilions, such as those of the large automakers, or in other exhibit halls, such as the Agricultural Group, the Electrical Building, and the General Exhibits Group. That arrangement worked quite well, as visitors took in science displays in the Hall of Science and then went on to see a working auto assembly line, a machine that produced banks that looked like little tin cans bearing the fair logo, and even an early form of television. New to the Century of Progress were mechanized dioramas, produced by the New York animatronics firm of Messmore and Damon. While dioramas—three-dimensional static displays of historic scenes or mechanical processes, for example—had been common at fairs, Messmore and Damon constructed dioramas with moving figures. In a diorama for the Baltimore and Ohio Railroad, which depicted the meeting at which the railroad was founded, lifelike figures moved and spoke. For International Harvester, the firm created a full-size mechanical cow that chewed its cud, blinked its eyes, moved its head and ears, switched its tail, breathed and mooed, and gave milk. For the General Motors Building, Messmore and Damon carried their fascination with robotics a step farther and created a mechanical Indian named Chief Pontiac, who answered visitors' questions about automobile production.[14]

Although the entertainment section of the Century of Progress, called the Midway, was not as well defined as it had been at some earlier fairs, there was still an abundance of entertainment. Most notably, the Streets of Paris featured replicas of Parisian houses and clubs, one of which headlined Sally Rand and her fan dance. Rand, a vaudeville entertainer, powdered her nude body completely white and did a provocative dance holding two large ostrich fans in front of her. At the end of the dance, she would raise the fans high above her head, revealing her whitened body, which some said bore a vague resemblance to a Greek or Roman sculpture. Although Rand's dance gravely offended some visitors and led to her arrest when she performed at a downtown night club, it was very popular and generated much free publicity for the Century of Progress. Other entertainment attractions included the Belgian Village, full of Old World charm; Enchanted Island, a five-acre playground for children; the popular Midget Village, which housed sixty midgets who put on diverse forms of

Dinosaurs made frequent appearances at world's fairs, particularly in connection with oil company exhibits. At the Century of Progress Exposition this dinosaur helped to promote the Sinclair Oil Company. (Photo courtesy of John E. Findling)

entertainment; Admiral Richard E. Byrd's ship; and *Wings of a Century*, an elaborate pageant on the history of transportation that was staged in a three thousand–seat outdoor amphitheater.[15]

Virtually absent from the Century of Progress were African Americans. A delegation of black civic leaders had met with Dawes soon after planning for the fair began and came away hopeful that there would be no discrimination in the employment or the treatment of black visitors. The black establishment endorsed the fair and urged African Americans to go and see it. In reality the Century of Progress was not color blind. Although the fair created many jobs, few went to African Americans during either the construction or the run of the fair. The only African American in the fair's

The Enchanted Island, a five-acre playground for children at the Century of Progress Exposition, featured a miniature railroad and the Magic Mountain, a glorified slide. (Photo by Kaufmann and Fabry Co., courtesy of John E. Findling)

management hierarchy headed the toilet concession, and most African Americans who did work at the fair cleaned toilets; a few others worked as maids, police, and demonstrators in a few exhibits.

Although the fair contained a handful of excellent African American exhibits from universities or the National Urban League, many other exhibits and entertainment attractions were racially degrading. The Sky Ride's two towers were named Amos and Andy, after the principal characters on the popular but racially stereotypical radio show. African Dips, a midway concession, offered visitors a chance to throw a ball through a hole; if they were successful, an African American was dropped into a tank of water. Another concession, Darkest Africa, titillated fairgoers with portrayals of Africans as brutal, sadistic savages.

In August 1933 fair managers sponsored Negro Day, which featured a parade, a beauty contest for Miss Bronze America, and a historical pageant in nearby Soldier Field. By that time the African American community was divided in its response to the fair; some supported it and others urged a boycott. In the end crowds were much smaller than anticipated, and the *Chicago Defender* reported, "Negro Day at Fair Flops." Before the 1934 season, the state legislature, mindful of African American complaints, passed a resolution stipulating that the fair not practice racial discrimination and providing a process for lodging complaints. The fair managers reacted by responding more diligently to complaints, but African Americans remained a minor presence at the fair.[16]

Late in the 1933 season, President Franklin Delano Roosevelt visited the Century of Progress, liked what he saw as a palliative for the depression, and suggested that the fair should reopen for a second season. The fair board was already considering that, and after the president's visit, it decided to operate the fair in 1934, with the hope that the additional revenue would enable the Century of Progress to pay off its original bondholders and to turn a profit.

The second season featured a simpler color scheme for the buildings, which used only ten colors instead of twenty-three, a larger number of foreign villages, all trying to capitalize on the success of the Streets of Paris, and the Ford Motor Company pavilion. Ford had not exhibited at the Century of Progress in 1933 because General Motors had announced in 1931 that its pavilion would have a working assembly line. That announcement annoyed Henry Ford, who had planned an assembly line for a Ford pavilion and disliked being upstaged by his chief rival. But the evident popularity of the Century of Progress in its first year drew Ford in for the second year. The Ford Building, which cost $5 million and featured regularly scheduled concerts by the Detroit Symphony Orchestra, was the most popular attraction at the fair in 1934.[17]

Before the fair had opened, *Fortune* magazine had predicted good attendance despite the depression: "[The Century of Progress] will attract many mid-western families who in more prosperous times would vacation in the mountains or at the seashore but who this summer will content themselves with piling into the family car and setting off to spend a few inexpensive days at the fairgrounds." The magazine's prediction was borne out. Over its two seasons the Century of Progress attracted some forty-eight million visitors and earned a modest profit of $160,000. The fact that those

A CENTURY OF PROGRESS! — CHICAGO 1933

The theme of progress is perfectly clear in this suggestive postcard from the Century of Progress Exposition. (Photo courtesy of John E. Findling)

figures could be attained during a catastrophic economic depression is a tribute to both the attractiveness of the exposition and the purposefulness of the businessmen who saw it as a means to check the nation's economic free fall.[18]

The success of the Century of Progress influenced civic leaders in San Diego, who wanted to duplicate the success of the 1915–16 Panama California Exposition and to help bring about economic recovery at the same time. This fair, the California Pacific International Exposition, ran from May 1935 to September 1936, with a three-month break in the winter. Preparation costs were low because the Balboa Park site and buildings of the earlier fair could be used. However, the fair managers added a Spanish Village, a theater, and a foreign representation area called the House of Pacific Relations, which consisted of fifteen cottages, each containing exhibits from a foreign country.

At the California Pacific Exposition, most of the exhibits were housed in a series of "palaces," exhibition halls devoted to science, foods and beverages, natural history, fine arts, better housing, and education. The House of

Charm featured exhibits on style and domestic arts and contained "everything that appeals to feminine taste and beauty."[19]

Once again one of the largest corporate exhibits was the Ford building, called the Ford Pavilion, which showcased the automobile production process. Walter Dorwin Teague designed the pavilion as a windowless structure composed of a circular entrance eighty-eight feet high and a larger, lower, circular main building with a central courtyard. The Ford Motor Company constructed its pavilion as a permanent building and donated it to the city as an exhibition center after the fair closed. A combination of indirect fluorescent and neon lighting highlighted the building at night. Elsewhere, an exhibit of model homes displayed miniaturized versions of typical 1930s housing styles on a raised platform that allowed the houses to be turned over, revealing the Victorian structures they replaced. Entertainment attractions along a midway included a frontier mining town, where one could occasionally place illegal bets, the Midget Village, fresh from its success in Chicago, and robots dancing with nude women at a place called the Zoro Gardens. More serious-minded visitors could see a Shakespeare play at a replica of the original Globe Theater, another permanent structure that became an important regional theater in southern California after the fair.

Although attendance at 6.75 million fell short of expectations, the fair did earn a tiny profit of $44,000. More important, like other depression era fairs, it helped San Diego's economy through the jobs it created; the millions of dollars brought in by visitors, concessionaires, and exhibitors; and the new buildings that remained in Balboa Park.[20]

Between the San Diego fair and the New York World's Fair of 1939–40, two important regional fairs took place: one in Dallas in 1936 and the other in Cleveland in 1936–37. Though neither involved enough foreign participation to qualify as a world's fair, both reflected major themes of the world's fairs between the wars: reliance on science, increasing corporate involvement, and persistent racial discrimination.

Plans for a Texas centennial celebration in 1936 had begun to form back in the 1920s, and by the early 1930s a number of state and local events were in the planning stages, including a large fair to be held in Dallas, the home of the annual state fair. The fairgrounds, with an architectural style that combined modernism with Spanish mission, Aztec, and Mayan motifs, was

These publicity labels advertised the important regional fairs held in Dallas (1936) and Cleveland (1936–37). (Photo courtesy of John E. Findling)

dominated by a tall tower topped by a star, symbolic of the Lone Star state. The tower stood at one end of a 700-foot-long reflecting pool called the Esplanade of Texas. Nearby were the Hall of Communications and the pavilions of Ford, General Motors, and Chrysler. The Texas Hall of Fame stood at the other end of the esplanade.

Much of the fair was devoted to agricultural and livestock exhibits, representing the traditional economic assets of the state. The state's history was dramatized in an extravagant pageant, *Cavalcade of Texas*, which was performed on a large outdoor stage. By the time the Texas Centennial Exposition opened on June 6, the most public controversy—whether the accomplishments of pioneer women should be represented by an abstract nude statue—had blown over, and the ceremonies went on amidst great fanfare.[21]

As a southern state, Texas had a considerable African American population in the 1930s, and by the early years of the decade, black leaders began to express interest in developing exhibits that would reflect the accomplishments of African Americans in the state. Efforts were made to secure money for black exhibits as part of the state's general appropriations for the fair and by selling fair bonds to wealthy black citizens, but both of those efforts failed. Black leaders, especially A. Maceo Smith, head of the Dallas Black Chamber of Commerce, finally succeeded in getting $100,000 of the $3 million federal appropriation for the fair designated for a Hall of Negro Life, with the stipulation that the exhibits were not to be used as a springboard for advocating black social progress. Instead, reflecting the tradition of Booker T. Washington and his accommodationist speech at the Atlanta fair of 1895, the exhibits would represent black arts and crafts, with a nod to black history.

At the fair local managers blocked African American participation. A black architect, John Blount, was denied permission to design the Hall of Negro Life; that job was given to the fair's architect in chief, George Dahl. Although the building was given a good location, between the General Motors pavilion and the Museum of Fine Arts, it was largely hidden behind a wall of shrubbery, setting it apart from the other fair buildings. Only a strong protest from Jesse D. Thomas, the federal government's manager of the hall, got "Colored" signs removed from the restrooms within the Hall of Negro Life (it was the only fair building to have integrated restrooms). Thomas also was able to persuade the operators of the sightseeing buses that circled the fairgrounds to take on African American passengers.

The Hall of Negro Life attracted about four hundred thousand visitors, about 60 percent of them white, during the run of the fair. Although most visitors enjoyed the pavilion and its exhibits, fair managers demolished the building and replaced it with one devoted to Latin American culture when the fair reopened the next year on a smaller scale as the Pan-American Exposition. The Hall of Negro Life was the only Texas Centennial Exposition building torn down before 1937.[22]

No such problems distressed the management of Cleveland's Great Lakes Exposition, which never had a pavilion devoted to African American culture. Like other fairs of the decade, that exposition, which celebrated the centennial of Cleveland's incorporation as a city, was seen as a way to revive the depression-ridden economy of northeastern Ohio. Under the leadership of prominent civic leader Dudley Blossom, some $1 million was raised by January 1936, and ground was broken in early March on a largely undeveloped site located between Municipal Stadium and the lakefront. Over the next four months, three thousand workers, including several hundred from the Works Projects Administration, turned the site into a pleasant fairgrounds dominated by industrially inspired, streamlined architecture and a heavy corporate presence. The centerpiece of the site was the Sherwin-Williams Plaza, paid for by the paint company of the same name, which featured a large band shell. Nearby was Radioland, housed in an existing public auditorium, from which nationally syndicated radio shows were broadcast, and Streets of the World, the international aspect of the fair. Streets of the World was a compact village of thirty replicas of structures from around the world; here cafés, shops, and exotic nightlife attractions were available.[23]

More standard exhibits included the Automotive Building, the Hall of Progress, which contained the federal government's exhibits, and other pavilions designed to remind visitors of the benefits of corporate capitalism. Other major venues included the Horticultural Building and Gardens and, on the lakeshore, the Marine Plaza, the Marine Theater, and the SS *Moses Cleveland*, a 350-foot Great Lakes merchant ship made into a nightclub. On the midway, next to Streets of the World, were other attractions, including Admiral Byrd's ship and World a Million Years Ago, both left over from the Century of Progress; a midget circus; a television display; the Front Page, a crime display featuring simulated executions; and Mammy's Cabin, billed as "a typical Southern log cabin, where colored women and children prepare spring chickens, waffle potatoes and biscuits for visitors who enjoy real southern cooking." At night electric lights created an artificial aurora borealis in the northern sky.[24]

The fair ran for one hundred days, attracted some four million visitors, and was successful enough to convince the management to revive it for a second season in 1937. That year, Ripley's Believe It or Not Odditorium, a very popular exhibit at the Century of Progress, was added, as was Billy Rose's *Aquacade*, a synchronized swimming show that would become the most popular entertainment attraction at the New York World's Fair of 1939–40.

The second season of the Great Lakes Exposition drew about three million visitors and encouraged civic leaders to make plans to develop the site into a permanent amusement and exhibit area. But after the Horticultural Building burned in 1941, interest flagged, and the site remained largely unused until the Rock and Roll Hall of Fame was opened there in 1996.[25]

Although New York City had not hosted a world's fair since the ill-fated Crystal Palace Exhibition of 1853, except for a very small undertaking in the Bronx in 1918 that was overshadowed by World War I, city leaders seeking economic remedies for the depression (and noting the success of the Century of Progress) began thinking about a fair in 1935. The year 1939 was seen as the most appropriate because that marked the 150th anniversary of George Washington's inauguration as the first president, an event that took place in New York City. Under the guidance of George McAneny, head of the Regional Planning Association, Grover Whalen, president of Schenley Distilleries and former police commissioner, and Percy Straus, president of Macy's department store, the fair was incorporated by September 1935, and a large board, dominated by business leaders, was formed. Initial public response, informed by a massive public relations campaign, was highly favorable. There were differing opinions within the fair's management over the style and theme of the fair: traditionalists wanted to build a more historically oriented fair, and functionalists were interested in a forward-looking exposition.

A number of prominent functionalists, including Michael Meredith Hare, secretary of the Municipal Art League, Harvey Wiley Corbett, an architect who had worked on the Century of Progress architectural commission, and Lewis Mumford, a cultural critic, developed plans for a "Fair of the Future." Such a fair would emphasize the opportunities that technology provides for "individual fulfillment and human progress." The planners urged the adoption of architectural and exhibitionary techniques that would reinforce the basic theme and suggested that corporate exhibits be required to comply with the theme. Walter Dorwin Teague, a leading industrial designer, and Robert Kohn, a past president of the American Institute of Architects (AIA), further refined the theme and came up with the motto "Building the World of Tomorrow." They also drew up an organizational plan for the site based on seven sectors corresponding to the varied functions of modern living, namely, government, production and distribution, transportation, communication, food, community interests, and amusement.[26]

In May 1936 a seven-member design board was appointed and given considerable latitude in establishing the fair's architectural style. Although that group, headed by the AIA president, Stephen F. Voorhees, was quite conservative, industrial designers such as Norman Bel Geddes, Raymond Loewy, and Henry Dreyfuss were able to make the fair's style modernistic, thanks to the influence of Walter Dorwin Teague.[27]

Robert Moses, New York City's parks commissioner, convinced the fair board to select Flushing Meadows as the site for the fair. Located in Queens, Flushing Meadows was a marshy place where the city dumped refuse. Moses, however, wanted to develop the site into a large park that would be the equal of Manhattan's Central Park. Some 1,216 acres of Flushing Meadows was set aside for the fair, making it second only to St. Louis as the largest site in the history of fairs and expositions.

The signature structures for the New York World's Fair, the Trylon and Perisphere, first appeared on the drawing boards in March 1937. The Trylon was a 610-foot-tall tower that held nothing and was connected by a 950-foot spiral walkway, the Helicline, to the Perisphere, which was 180 feet in diameter, in which the theme exhibit of the fair, Democracity, was displayed. Along Constitution Avenue, the main street of the fair, stood most of the foreign pavilions. Every major nation except Germany was present for the 1939 season. The pavilion of the Soviet Union, with its 180-foot-tall marble pillar, on which stood a 79-foot-tall sculpture of a Soviet worker, was the most impressive.

The architecture of the fair, with its strong emphasis on geometric lines and figures in the form of domes, towers, pylons, and pyramidal shapes, continued the modern style influenced by art deco, which had dominated the Century of Progress. Predominantly windowless walls were painted in bright colors or made attractive by the effective use of various forms of lighting. Some buildings displayed neoclassical ornamental elements, which, when combined with the modernism quite apparent elsewhere, led one critic to use the descriptive term "Beaux-Arts moderne" to describe the overall look.[28]

Among the exhibitors at the fair were some of the largest corporations in the United States, including all the major automobile manufacturers, American Telephone & Telegraph (AT&T), Kodak, U.S. Steel, the Radio Corporation of America (RCA), which displayed television, and Westinghouse, whose robot, Elecktro the Moto-Man, could smoke cigarettes. General Motors' 35,000-square-foot exhibit, Futurama, was the most popular. Visitors sat in moving chairs and rode slowly by Norman Bel Geddes's vision of the country in 1960, which emphasized a carefully designed highway system "with its seven lanes accommodating traffic at designated speeds of 50, 75 and 100 miles an hour . . . engineered for easy grades and for curves that require no reduction in speed." The automobile corpora-

The Trylon and Perisphere at the New York World's Fair of 1939–40 are the most recognizable symbols of all world's fairs. (Photo courtesy of John E. Findling)

tion, mindful of the products it made, "[sought] to show that highway progress will be an even more important factor in the world of tomorrow than it has been in the world of yesterday." Not only were the highways of 1960 carefully engineered, but also the cities of 1960 had fallen under the hand of science: "The city of 1960 has abundant sunshine, fresh air, fine green parkways, recreational and civic centers—all the result of thoughtful planning and design." Essayist E. B. White, writing in the *New Yorker*, mused about Futurama:

When night falls . . . , and you lean back in the cushioned chairs (yourself in motion and the world so still) and hear (from the depths of the chair) the soft electric assurance of a better life—the life which rests on wheels alone—there is a strong, sweet poison which infects the blood. I didn't want to wake up. I liked 1960 in a purple light, going a hundred miles an hour around impossible turns ever onward toward the certified cities of the flawless future.[29]

The theme exhibit, Democracity, was equally elaborate and had significant political overtones. Henry Dreyfuss designed a huge diorama of a utopian futuristic urban space set in the year 2039 for the interior of the Perisphere. Some eight thousand visitors an hour looked down from two circular moving sidewalks on the balcony that surrounded the diorama. In the six-minute show, day changed to night and back to day, and the specter of one thousand marching people (presumably in defense of democracy) was first heard and then seen in the sky through an image projected on the ceiling.[30]

The Amusement Zone occupied 280 acres of the site and in 1939 included a freak show called *We Humans*. The guidebook noted that the attraction was so "strange and terrifying it couldn't be described." The most successful attraction was Billy Rose's *Aquacade*, an elaborate swimming show starring former Olympians Eleanor Holm and Johnny Weismuller and a cast of synchronized swimmers. In 1940 the Amusement Zone was renamed the Great White Way, and Buster Crabbe replaced Johnny Weismuller as Eleanor Holm's partner in the *Aquacade*. *We Humans* was no longer an attraction, but the tethered Parachute Jump, a hit in 1939, remained popular. Those seeking erotic titillation could find it in the Living Magazine Covers exhibit, where "faces and figures of models made famous by artists for magazine covers are spotlighted in a sparkling show of feminine pulchritude softened by trick lighting."[31]

Although the African Dip concession did not make an appearance at the New York World's Fair, African Americans had been concerned about their treatment at the fair ever since Grover Whalen became head of the world's fair commission. Whalen, a political conservative, had been criticized for flattering Benito Mussolini and the Italian fascist party during his trip to Italy to secure that country's participation in the fair. The National Association for the Advancement of Colored People (NAACP) demanded that civil rights laws be enforced and that discriminatory employment practices be forbidden. But few African Americans found work at the site during the construction of the fair, and the fair management rejected complaints about unfair treatment by contractors.

With the help of Mayor Fiorello La Guardia, the black employment situation improved somewhat, although most blacks worked in menial jobs. More than four hundred frustrated African Americans picketed just outside the gates during the opening ceremonies on April 30, 1939. Later, as the European war began and the prospect of U.S. involvement became more likely, fair officials realized the importance of unified support for the war,

At the New York World's Fair in 1940, Negro Week featured a wide array of
African American entertainment, including this women's chorus. (Photo courtesy
of John E. Findling)

including that of African Americans. For the 1940 season the Soviet pavilion was replaced by a space called the American Common; here ethnic festivals were staged, including a Negro Week, which was highlighted by
W. E. B. DuBois's opening day speech and a wide selection of musical performances.[32]

Despite the outbreak of war in Europe, the managers of the New York
World's Fair decided to open their fair for a second season. The admission
price was reduced from seventy-five cents to fifty cents, the international
flavor of the fair was reduced, and visitors instead were encouraged to
"travel America." Because of the war in Europe, a number of foreign nations did not participate in 1940, but the American Common and its culturally diverse events all supported the new theme of the fair: "For Peace
and Freedom." Denmark withdrew its exhibit from the Hall of Nations and
was replaced by Iraq, while an American organization, the Friends of Nor-
way, sustained that country's presence at the fair. Despite bad weather and

what observers called a "loss of spirit," just over nineteen million visitors came to the fair in 1940. That year the fair showed a $5 million profit, but it was not enough to offset the huge losses from 1939, and the final balance sheet showed a shortfall of $18.7 million. No funds were left to complete Robert Moses's planned improvements to Flushing Meadows Park, and the fair's structures, including the Trylon and Perisphere, were torn down and their scrap steel was donated to the war effort.[33]

Despite its financial difficulties and the gloom brought on by the war in Europe, the New York World's Fair has become, over the years, the most nostalgically remembered American exposition. The Trylon and Perisphere are the best known world's fair icons, E. L. Doctorow and David Gelernter both have written novels set in and around the fair, and souvenirs from the fair fetch very high prices. The American actor Jason Robards, in an interview related to his work as narrator of a 1984 television documentary about the fair, recalled that he had visited the fair as a ten-year-old boy in 1939 and said: "I think it must have stayed with every child who saw it. Every child who, grown up now, seeing home movies or finding in a drawer a blue-and-white button or souvenir postcard, wishes, just for a moment, that he could go back to the future—to that 'World of Tomorrow' now contained forever in a lost American yesterday."[34]

On the other side of the United States, another fair was held at the same time as the New York World's Fair—the Golden Gate International Exposition. It was yet another fair that originated as a way to combat the Great Depression. Following the construction of the Golden Gate and San Francisco–Oakland Bay bridges, local civic leaders thought that a world's fair would be a fine way to continue providing jobs in a quasi–public works setting, especially since San Francisco had already hosted fairs in 1894 and 1915.

Treasure Island, in San Francisco Bay, was chosen as the fair site. A manmade island next to Yerba Buena Island, Treasure Island was built in about a year and a half in the early 1930s with 287,000 tons of rock and 20 million cubic feet of sand. When completed, the island contained four hundred acres in a rectangular shape about fifty-five hundred by thirty-four hundred feet and had cost $3.72 million in Works Projects Administration funds. To prepare the island for the fair, engineers lowered the salt water table and leached the black sandy soil for four months to desalinize it. Then workers spread one hundred thousand cubic yards of loam from the Sacramento

Valley and installed a sprinkler system. Four thousand trees, some as much as seventy feet tall, were planted, along with forty thousand shrubs, small trees, and tropical grasses. The role of the exposition in alleviating unemployment was clear: twelve hundred workers were hired to plant millions of flowers that had been grown in San Francisco's Golden Gate Park. An additional 435,000 bulbs were planted according to a predetermined color scheme. Fairgoers could reach the island either by ferry or by car across the new San Francisco–Oakland Bay bridge, and the fairgrounds provided ample parking.[35]

97

In keeping with their decision to focus on the nations that ringed the Pacific Basin, fair planners opted for an eclectic exoticism in the architectural design. Visitors entered the main gate between two tall elephant towers, modeled after those at Angkor Wat, an ancient Cambodian temple. Once inside the grounds, fairgoers could wander through a maze of courts that made up the organization of the site. The principal court, the Court of Honor, featured the 400-foot-tall Tower of the Sun, which some critics compared with a science fiction version of a large rocket ship. Other courts included reflecting pools, outdoor sculpture, and arched colonnades. Solid walls around the outside of each court protected fairgoers from the cool breezes off the water. The architecture throughout the fair reflected the growing trend toward modernization, although Asian ornamental elements and pastel colors softened the geometrical severity of many of the buildings.

As they had at the Century of Progress Exposition, color and light played important roles in the aesthetics of the Golden Gate International Exposition. The director of color, Jesse E. Stanton, developed a scheme that utilized nineteen colors based on the natural hues of the Pacific coast and barred the use of all other colors except those customarily associated with a corporate sponsor. In the inner courts, the pastel colors, often enhanced by indirect lighting, were harmonized with the flowers. A team of illumination engineers, headed by A. F. Dickerson, employed 10,000 colored floodlights, 130 searchlights, and 300 ultraviolet lamps. Mixing primary colors created other colors, and the ultraviolet lights were used with luminescent paints on murals to make them glow in the dark. The fair's fountains were bathed in colored lights, and twenty-four military searchlights created a panoramic backdrop of color that was visible for one hundred miles.[36]

Exhibits, which were housed in the various structures that formed each court, resembled those at the New York World's Fair but frequently were

This souvenir ticket stub from San Francisco's Golden Gate International Exposition of 1939 shows the fair's signature structure, the Tower of the Sun, and the two bridges recently completed that linked San Francisco with nearby areas. (Photo courtesy of John E. Findling)

less elaborate. Visitors could see television, a model of the San Francisco of 1999, and robots performing assorted tasks. Each of the major automobile manufacturers was present, but only Ford had its own pavilion. Chrysler and General Motors mounted exhibits in Vacationland, one of the larger exhibit halls. Most of the western states and a number of California counties also had their own exhibits. An art exhibit featured $40 million worth of classic European paintings, as well as displays of Pacific Rim art, contemporary art, and decorative art. Women and African Americans had no prominent place at the fair, although fair managers did create a women's board headed by Hazel Pedlar Faulkner. Her task was to interest women in the features of the exposition and to arrange for distinguished women visitors to be appropriately recognized. Although African Americans had no presence, the fair did suggest in a number of ways that Asian and Latin American civilizations would benefit from the "blessings" of American commercial hegemony.[37]

An entertainment area, called the Gayway, contained the usual midway attractions, including Sally Rand, now managing a western Nude Ranch, a roller coaster, a diving bell that took visitors to the bottom of a large fish tank, and a group of babies in incubators. The most spectacular entertainment was a pageant called the *Cavalcade of the Golden West,* which had a cast of two hundred actors and two hundred animals portraying the history of the American West.

Like the New York World's Fair, the Golden Gate International Exposition ran for two seasons. Before it closed on September 29, 1940, the fair had attracted over seventeen million visitors and had breathed fresh life into dreams of an American empire in the Pacific Basin. When the fair ended, Europe was again at war, and Treasure Island was turned over to the federal government for use as a naval aviation station.[38]

Undoubtedly the fairs of the 1930s brightened America's mood during the Great Depression. By alternately focusing attention on America's past achievements and on its future possibilities, the fairs diverted the public from the hard times of the decade. They injected hope and optimism into a nation suffering from economic collapse. Historians often ask why the United States pulled out of the depression and avoided political revolution. Perhaps the great fairs of the era are part of the answer.

4
FAIRS IN THE ATOMIC AGE

ollowing World War II, no world's fairs were held in the United States until the Century 21 Exposition in Seattle in 1962. The adjustment back to civilian life in the United States, the tensions of the early cold war years, and, perhaps, the debt-ridden outcome of the New York World's Fair of 1939–40 all contributed to a reluctance to stage a postwar fair in America.

The Brussels Universal Exposition of 1958, however, did generate a great deal of interest in the United States. That exposition, the first major fair held anywhere since the war, was highlighted by a cold war–style confrontation between the Soviet Union and the United States. Many fairgoers from the United States felt that the Soviet Pavilion, which displayed impressive amounts of military and space-related hardware, including a Sputnik model, represented that nation's image more successfully than did the popular culture–oriented U.S. Pavilion. The Eisenhower administration was embarrassed by the U.S. presence at the Brussels fair, did its best to put a positive spin on it, and resolved not to let the country end up in such a position again.

With the Century 21 Exposition the city of Seattle gave the United States the opportunity to improve on its showing in Brussels. In the mid-1950s a number of Seattle civic leaders began to talk about a fair in 1959 to celebrate the fiftieth anniversary of the Alaska-Yukon-Pacific Exposition and to boost the flagging economy of the city in the wake of layoffs by the giant aircraft manufacturer, Boeing. Among them was Alfred Rochester, president of the Seattle City Council, who had worked at the A-Y-P as a teenager. In February 1955 fair enthusiasts approached the state legislature, which formed a commission, headed by Eddie Carlson, a hotel executive, to study the economic feasibility of the idea. In the fall of 1956 the commission recommended that a Festival of the West be held from July through October in 1960 and 1961, since there was not enough time to prepare an exposition for 1959. In November 1956 Seattle voters approved a $7.5 million bond issue to acquire land and to begin building the fair at a site near the center of the city. An important aspect of that bond issue was the renovation of the civic auditorium into an elegant opera house that could be used for the most important cultural events of the exposition. In early 1957 the legislature created a world's fair commission, and Governor Victor Rosselini, working with an informal group of supporters, selected the name "Century 21 Exposition."[1]

In March 1957 the commission appointed Ewen Dingwall, the executive director of the Washington State Research Council, as director of the Century 21 Exposition. Later that year a young Seattle architect, Clayton Young, became Dingwall's assistant and helped the director choose a Design Standards Advisory Board, which was composed of a number of local architects as well as Lawrence Halperin of San Francisco and Minora Yamasaki of Detroit.[2]

The Soviet Union's successful orbiting of Sputnik in October 1957 inadvertently provided a boost and a theme for the Seattle fair. Could the United States compete with the Soviet Union on America's home ground? Could the United States overcome its failures in space during the months after Sputnik? Those questions put Seattle's fair planners to the test and forced them to reflect on the history of recent American fairs, especially the Century of Progress Exposition in 1933, where the Hall of Science had been the principal exhibit building, and the New York World's Fair of 1939–40, where science's role in building the world of tomorrow had been an important focal point. Could the Seattle exposition restore the American public's confidence in science?

While continuing their soul-searching, Century 21 planners went to Washington, D.C., to seek federal funding for their fair, working through influential Senator Warren B. Magnuson. While there they heard that leaders of the American scientific community were in the city for a conference of the American Association for the Advancement of Science. Some of the scientists were promoting the idea of a "world's fair of science" as a way to meet the Soviet challenge. A dinner was hastily arranged, and Century 21 officials and a number of prominent scientists agreed in principle to use the Seattle fair as a showcase for U.S. scientific achievements. That development also added weight to Seattle's request that Congress help fund the fair. Even so, the fight for funding in Washington, D.C., was difficult, and not until late 1959 did Congress appropriate funds for the Century 21 Exposition.[3]

By that time the fair's run had been rescheduled for 1961–62. To secure the sanction of the Bureau Internationale des Expositions (BIE), the international body that had been established earlier in the 1920s to regulate the frequency of world's fairs, the planners made Century 21 a one-season, six-month exposition, which allowed it to garner much more foreign participation. Some forty-nine nations and the city of West Berlin were present at the fair, and nearly all produced exhibits that supported its main science-oriented themes. In addition a number of pavilions represented various western states and Canadian provinces, as well as some of America's leading corporations, which were seeking to take advantage of the rapidly growing consumer culture in the postwar United States.[4]

The seventy-four-acre site, which cost $77 million to develop, was remarkable because, unlike past fairs, some 75 percent of the construction was permanent. With the help of the Disney corporation, which designed much of the landscaping, the rectangular site was laid out so that three groups of permanent buildings formed three sides of the fairgrounds. On one side was the newly renovated auditorium, now the Opera House, along with a parking garage, theater, and fine arts exhibit hall. On a second side was an eighteen thousand–seat coliseum and several adjacent exhibition halls. On the third side was the U.S. Science Pavilion, with auxiliary buildings and a plaza filled with decorative fountains. Another permanent structure was the Space Needle, a privately funded tower 606 feet high with a revolving spaceship-style restaurant at its top. Designed by John Graham and Company and Victor Steinbruck, it was considered Seattle's Eiffel Tower and remains today the city's most distinctive landmark.[5]

The best architectural work, according to most critics, was done by Minora Yamasaki, a Japanese American, who, with his family, had been interned in relocation camps set up by the federal government during World War II. Yamasaki suggested that the frame and shell of the old auditorium

This aerial view of the 1962 Century 21 Exposition shows the Space Needle and the layout of the fair site with downtown Seattle in the background. (Photo courtesy of the Museum of History and Industry, Seattle)

were sound and that a new auditorium could be built around them. However, Yamasaki is best remembered for the U.S. Science Pavilion, a graceful, airy structure with stylized Gothic arches and a plaza featuring fountains and flowers.[6]

Within the U.S. Science Pavilion, the exhibit space was divided into six areas. The first space that visitors encountered was devoted to an innovative film by Charles Eames. Projected by seven cameras on a long, curved wall, the film portrayed the development and complexity of science through a series of rapidly changing images. Another section of the six-part exhibit that focused on science education, the Spacearium, used planetarium-like techniques to take visitors on a journey into space. In an adjoining building was the $2 million National Aeronautics and Space Administration exhibit, which featured models of satellites, displays of tracking stations, and the

Inside the U.S. Science Pavilion, fairgoers could learn much about the current state of science in America. (Photo courtesy of the Museum of History and Industry, Seattle)

module that had carried astronaut Alan Shepard on the first U.S. suborbital spaceflight in 1961.

It was not lost on critics that the "space Gothic" architecture of the U.S. Science Pavilion had religious connotations, and fair planners were conscious of an ongoing national debate between science and religion. Directly across from the U.S. Science Pavilion, the Christian Witness Pavilion helped to further that debate. Christian Witness, a local committee of Protestant churches, embellished its pavilion with wooden arches and a cross. Inside, visitors watched a film titled *Redeemed*, which was controversial and confusing, lacked a clear narrative, and tried to convey its point by means of modernistic montages of space-age Christianity. No less important and more interesting to fairgoers was the Sermons from Science Pavilion, which the Moody Bible Institute created as part of its ongoing effort to convince Americans that science and religion were compatible ways of knowing about the universe. By the end of the fair, nothing was settled, but Century 21 had "extended a running exchange" in a positive and entertaining manner.[7]

The entertainment zone of Century 21, known as the Gayway, had twenty rides, a fun house, and one terminal of a cable car ride across the fairgrounds. Nearby was Show Street, billed as an adult entertainment zone. Visitors could take in *Paradise International,* an extravagant musical revue staged by Gracie Harrison; *Backstage USA,* a stage show seen from backstage; and Paris Spectacular, a wax museum. Following the example of the Century of Progress and the New York World's Fair, more risqué entertainment was offered as well, including Planet Eve, in which topless showgirls seduced performers dressed as astronauts.[8]

The Century 21 Exposition attracted some ten million visitors and earned enough money to cover its costs. The fair was a pleasant experience for most, on a site far more compact than Brussels' 500 acres and New York's 646 acres. Russell Lynes, a popular culture critic for *Harper's,* captured the spirit of the fair:

The Fair smiles. In fact it smiles rather more than it does anything else and its smile is ingratiating. It is modest without being coy, and it is pretty without being seductive. It is friendly and gay and feels like a girl in a flowered hat. Compared with most world's fairs, indeed with any that I can think of, it is polite, perky, rather than pretentious, and lovable rather than overwhelming.[9]

Century 21 also left a significant legacy to its host city. A monorail connecting the fairgrounds to downtown Seattle, a distance of 1.2 miles, did not become the prototype of urban mass transit, as some had hoped, but remains today as a tourist attraction. A private corporation was formed to handle the transition of the site and its buildings from fair to postfair use, but eventually it failed, and the job was assumed by the city, which contracted its operation to a company called Greater Seattle, Inc. The U.S. Science Pavilion became the Pacific Science Center, the British pavilion was made into a branch of the Seattle Art Museum, where visiting exhibitions currently are displayed, and the Coliseum became the home of the city's professional basketball and hockey franchises.[10]

If the Seattle fair was notable for its exhibitionary and financial success, the New York World's Fair of 1964–65 met just the opposite fate. A large, ram-

The Unisphere, a large stylized globe, was meant to illustrate the theme of "Peace Through Understanding" at the New York World's Fair of 1964–65. (Photo courtesy of John E. Findling)

bling, unfocused exposition, the New York fair attracted far more attention for its perpetual financial woes than for anything it had to offer visitors.

The idea for a second New York fair surfaced about 1958. Robert Kopple, a lawyer, first suggested such an event, and Charles Preusse, a city official, and Thomas Duggan, a public relations expert, promoted Kopple's idea. The year 1964 was chosen to celebrate the tercentenary of New York becoming an English colony. Robert Moses, then chairman of the Triborough Bridge and Transit Authority, was selected as the president of the fair board. The choice seemed fitting because he had been a major promoter of the 1939–40 New York World's Fair, the profits from which he had hoped to use to develop Flushing Meadows as a large city park. When the 1939–40 fair lost money, that project proved impossible, and to Moses another fair at the same site must have seemed like a heaven-sent opportunity.

A site plan, similar to but more simplified than that of the earlier fair, was adopted. From the Unisphere, a huge metal globe that was the signature structure of the fair and meant to portray the theme of the fair, "Peace Through Understanding," avenues radiated outward in various directions, taking visitors to different zones: transportation, industry, government, and amusement. The government zone, divided into international and federal and state areas, was nearest the Unisphere.[11]

The New York World's Fair might have benefited from broader foreign participation, but Moses, who referred to the BIE as "three little men in a cheap hotel room in Paris," was not willing to fashion the fair along BIE guidelines. The BIE refused to sanction Moses's fair, and most major European nations chose not to participate in any official way. There were, however, numerous privately sponsored foreign exhibits, as well as others that were jointly sponsored by government and private interests. For the first time developing nations enjoyed a significant presence at an American fair, with exhibits from many newly independent Asian and African nations.[12]

More than ever the fair was oriented toward commercial or corporate pavilions, and those competed with one another for design prominence. The 400-foot-long Bell System Pavilion, designed by the firm of Harrison and Abramovitz, appeared to float thirty-five feet above the Pool of Industry, while Eero Saarinen's design for IBM resulted in an elevated, egg-shaped pavilion. Other pavilions utilized inflated roofs, lightweight plastic or fiberglass wall panels, or suspended roof or wall systems. A number of entertainment venues, including Picturesque Belgium, Lowenbrau Gardens, and Bourbon Street New Orleans, replicated traditional architectural styles appropriate to their themes, as did a number of church-sponsored pavilions. Architectural critic Vincent J. Scully Jr. was not impressed, however. Writing in *Life*, Scully concluded that the fair "ha[d] nothing creative in its layout; . . . [it uses] the same zombie ground plan that was already dead for the 1939 World's Fair." As for individual pavilions, Scully termed the IBM Pavilion "a huge eagle's egg, heavily laid on a thicket," and the General Motors effort "a Detroit-style marriage between a tailfin and a hubcap."[13]

Despite Scully's opinion, the General Motors Pavilion was the largest and most popular attraction at the fair, much as it had been in 1939–40. Presenting an updated version of its earlier exhibit, Futurama, it showed visitors a trip to the moon, underwater resorts, and applications of solar energy and made ample use of the art of animatronics, or lifelike talking ro-

Whether or not visitors thought that the roof of the IBM Pavilion at the New York World's Fair looked like a large egg, they still enjoyed the state-of-the-art exhibits inside. (Photo courtesy of John E. Findling)

bots. The Ford exhibit was prepared by the Walt Disney studio and amounted to what Scully called "phony reality . . . that we all too readily accept in place of the true." Chrysler's exhibit included an oversized working engine that visitors could walk through and a clever zoo featuring animals made out of automobile parts. There were many other commercial pavilions as well. Coca-Cola and Pepsi competed for the soft drink market, IBM staged a computer show, the Formica House had exterior walls made of the product, and National Cash Register demonstrated the wonders of modern record keeping. Because of the lack of official sanction, the fair's foreign exhibits were, for the most part, small and centered around commercial products, a few antiquities, or restaurants.[14]

Other popular exhibits included the Hall of Free Enterprise, sponsored by the American Economic Foundation, which promoted free market enterprise and even offered an accredited graduate course in economics in a two-week session, sponsored by Adelphi University. The U.S. Pavilion cost

Sinclair Oil brought back new and improved animatronic dinosaurs at the New York World's Fair in 1964–65. (Photo courtesy of John E. Findling)

$17 million, one of the largest amounts of federal money ever spent on an American fair. It included two films, one on immigration and one on U.S. history and its possible future, and exhibits under the rubrics of "Challenge for Freedom" and "Challenge of a Peaceful World," which emphasized organizations and topics such as the Peace Corps and progress in space exploration. The New York City exhibit, housed in one of the two structures left over from the 1939–40 fair, included a 180 foot by 100 foot scale model of the city.[15]

The highlight of the fine arts display was Michelangelo's sculpture *La Pietà*, which was being shown for the first time outside Vatican City. Its packing and shipping to the Vatican Pavilion generated a great deal of publicity and doubtless brought additional visitors out to Flushing Meadows. In addition, visitors were impressed by the exhibit at the Spanish Pavilion that featured works by artists ranging from El Greco to Salvador Dali. Unlike most previous fairs, the New York World's Fair did not have a fine arts pavilion, although the guidebook included a section on New York's many art museums.[16]

Because Robert Moses did not care for most typical amusement features, the fair had only a limited number of rides, although visitors could visit a wax museum, a porpoise show, and a puppet show titled *Les Poupées de Paris*. In addition, Picturesque Belgium included replicas of more than one hundred houses, a fifteenth-century church, a city hall, and a canal, all on a four-acre site. Belgium had the largest international presence at the fair, and visitors had to pay an extra $1.25 to see that exhibit. The U.S. Rubber Company's contribution was an eighty-foot-tall Ferris Wheel disguised as a huge tire, where for twenty-five cents a visitor could ride in one of twenty-four gondolas moving around the circumference of the tire. Unlike the Century of Progress Exposition, the New York World's Fair of 1939–40, and Seattle's Century 21 Exposition, this New York World's Fair did not tolerate adult entertainment. In May 1965 fair security personnel closed a strip show in the Bourbon Street New Orleans attraction, although the stripper had left the stage still well attired, once in a cocktail dress, once in an "oversized bikini." Rumors had spread that such entertainment would be allowed, since *Dancing Waters*, another musical show, had hired professional striptease dancer Sherry Britton, but she was also barred from performing.[17]

By 1964 the civil rights movement in the United States was near its peak of activity, both on the streets and in Congress. Martin Luther King Jr.'s advocacy of nonviolent demonstrations had captured the imagination of the movement, and rallies, marches, and sit-ins were commonplace at most public gatherings. Opening Day of the New York World's Fair was no exception. With the knowledge that President Lyndon B. Johnson would be present, hundreds of demonstrators, recalling the opening of the 1939 fair, gathered both inside and outside of the fairgrounds. Those inside staged sit-ins in front of various stairways and entrances and heckled Johnson as he dedicated the U.S. Pavilion. About three hundred demonstrators were arrested, and a good deal of public hostility was ventilated. One white woman was heard to admonish her child: "When I say step on them, step on them!"[18]

Despite those distractions, the fair's financial condition was soon receiving the most attention in newspapers and magazines. Negative publicity resulting from the civil rights protests, along with bad weather, put the fair in a fiscal dilemma from which it never recovered. Although Robert Moses

The U.S. Rubber Company put a new spin on Ferris Wheel design for the New York World's Fair. (Photo courtesy of John E. Findling)

had optimistically predicted a 1964 attendance of between forty and fifty million, the final count registered just twenty-seven million, leaving fair officials with a $20 million deficit. New York City officials were upset when Moses announced that the city would not receive any of the $24 million it had spent on behalf of the fair, nor would there be enough money to carry out the park development that had been planned. Five bankers resigned from the fair's finance committee, claiming that Moses never provided them with enough information to do their job, and city officials called for an outside audit of the fair's books.[19]

From the beginning a second season for the fair had been planned, and fair officials began looking for ways to cut operating costs and to attract more visitors in 1965. Hoping to benefit from word-of-mouth recommendations, the fair board slashed its advertising budget and studied the mistakes of 1964, such as long lines at restaurants and the underutilized Amusement Zone. Strong consideration was given to reducing the $2 gen-

eral admission cost ($1 for children) by instituting a family rate, an idea fa-
vored by Mayor Robert Wagner. In the end, however, Moses succeeded in
pushing through an increase in the daily admission fee to $2.50 and $1.50.
Many exhibitors refurbished or improved their exhibits for 1965, and there
were some entirely new attractions, including one honoring the life of
Winston Churchill, who had recently died. A number of smaller corporate
exhibitors that had failed financially in 1964 were gone, as were a few un-
profitable amusement attractions, including *Ice-travaganza*, a glitzy and expensive ice show sponsored by New York City.[20]

Despite economic predictions that the fair would have to generate $97.4
million in revenue in its second season, some 50 percent more than in
1964, to break even, fair officials remained optimistic about the 1965 version
of the fair. They publicized the fact that exhibitors had spent $7 million on
new or remodeled exhibits and that the number of restaurants had been increased from 111 to 198, allowing thirty-eight thousand visitors to be served
at any one time. A new attraction, People to People, was billed as a community fiesta, with folk dancing and singing in colorful tents, along with
arts and crafts displays. When the fair closed in October 1965, another
twenty-four million visitors had been counted, and another $1 million had
been added to the deficit. The city, however, had registered a 6 to 8 percent
increase in restaurant trade, a 4 percent increase in retail sales, and a small
increase in hotel occupancy rates.[21]

As the demolition of more than one hundred structures proceeded at
Flushing Meadows, New Yorkers asked themselves why the fair had been
such a financial failure. Much of the blame was directed at Robert Moses,
whose involvement in many other civic projects left him little time for the
fair, and whose autocratic manner made him difficult to work with. He and
the other fair officials ignored the advice of architects and fair experts; rejected opportunities for cooperation with local government officials, the
press, and the BIE; and failed to use sound business practices in their management of the exposition. Those problems led to negative press reports
about the fair, which in turn hurt attendance. Never again has such a large-
scale exposition been attempted in the United States.[22]

In the wake of the New York World's Fair came Alaska '67, a small fair intended to celebrate the centennial of the purchase of Alaska from Russia.

Situated on a forty-acre site near the Chena River in downtown Fairbanks, Alaska '67 was scheduled to run from May 27 until September 10 and to include many exhibits related to the state's heritage and its Eskimo, Tlingit, and Athabascan cultures. In addition, there was to be a North to the Future pavilion with foreign exhibits, a federal government pavilion, and a 227-foot stern-wheeler, the *Nenana*, built in 1933.

The fair opened on schedule, but constant rain during the latter half of July brought the Chena River nine feet over flood stage, flooding downtown Fairbanks and the fairgrounds. The flood caused five deaths and over $200 million in property damage and was the worst disaster in Fairbanks history. Damage at the fair's site was so extensive that it never reopened.[23]

Meanwhile plans were under way for HemisFair '68, a fair that opened in 1968 in San Antonio, Texas. The idea for HemisFair was first broached in 1959 by local businessman Jerome Harris, who urged an international fair with a Latin American focus to spark a flat economy and to promote interest in San Antonio's heritage. The idea caught on with local officials, who saw in it a way to spur their urban renewal program and to acquire a modern convention, amusement, and educational complex near the city's center. Moreover, U.S. policy toward Latin America had changed during the 1960s, moving away from a blatant anticommunism toward a more mutually satisfactory commercial relationship. That shift could be seen in such measures as the Alliance for Progress, which was initiated by the Kennedy administration in 1961. The Century 21 Exposition in Seattle had paid some attention to the desirability of Latin American markets, but it made even more sense for a San Antonio fair to emphasize its linkage with Hispanic America and its people. In addition, with the United States already fighting a war in Vietnam, it was good politics to encourage friendships in other parts of the world. In 1962 Congressman Henry B. Gonzalez, a Democrat from Texas, endorsed the idea of a Fair for the Americas, and Governor John B. Connally pledged to secure exhibitors, funding, and official sanction. Once civic leaders agreed to link the fair with urban renewal, a downtown site was a certainty, and soon a ninety-two-acre site just east of downtown was selected. The site was ideal because it had already been earmarked for renewal and because the Paseo del Rio—a riverwalk project that dated back to the 1930s—could be extended into it. A feasibil-

HemisFair '68 in San Antonio sported many impressive fountains because of its connection with the city's Paseo del Rio urban renewal project. (Photo courtesy of John E. Findling)

ity study the following year reported favorably on the potential economic benefits of the proposed fair, and once funding was assured through a successful bond issue and pledges of support from area businesses, work began.

A site plan roughly similar to that used in Seattle was adopted, in which permanent buildings would be located around the perimeter of the site, and a 622-foot-tall tower, the Tower of the Americas, would mark the center. At HemisFair the plan worked outward from the Tower of the Americas in roughly concentric triangles, with the entertainment zone, Fiesta Island, closest to the tower, followed by the waterway, smaller exhibits, and on the perimeter large, permanent structures, including the Texas Pavilion (which became the Institute for Texan Cultures), the U.S. Pavilion, and the convention center. In addition architects were able to save and to reuse some twenty-seven older buildings (most served as fair offices, shops, and restaurants) as well as a large number of existing trees.

HemisFair provided space in prefabricated modular buildings for the twenty-four nations, nineteen corporations, and twelve organizations that mounted exhibits and displays. A system of elevated walkways and a mini-monorail helped people get from one part of the site to another, and a channel from the San Antonio River was built into the site and scenically adorned with limestone rock walls, trees, and miniature waterfalls. Some parts of the site were accessible by gondola, and visitors could enjoy a meal on one of several dining barges.[24]

The U.S. exhibit, Confluence U.S.A., best expressed the fair's theme of cultural diversity. In static exhibits and a three-screen film, the history and impact of immigration into the United States was presented. Another major part of Confluence U.S.A., mounted in the convention center's exhibit hall, traced humanity's relationship with the universe over time and into the future.[25]

Although HemisFair attracted 6.4 million visitors and was favorably reviewed by critics and visitors alike, it nevertheless ended with a $5 million loss. Construction costs were higher than anticipated, and advance publicity was limited because of the 1967 exposition in Montreal and the BIE's stipulation that a fair could not advertise itself while another was in progress. Rainy weather and the fear of racially focused urban violence, prevalent during the civil rights movement in many American cities during the 1960s, may have conspired to reduce attendance, as did a boycott instigated by the activist organization La Raza Unidad, which accused HemisFair of discriminatory employment practices against Mexican Americans.

Nevertheless, HemisFair did succeed in boosting the city's economy, providing short-term jobs for eight thousand people, and leaving several important buildings as its legacy. In 1969 the site reopened as a permanent amusement park called Fiestaland. Over the longer term HemisFair made urban renewal a focus of the city's concerns and inaugurated an era of much increased tourist and convention activity.[26]

The thematic eclecticism of the fairs held in the Atomic Age took another spin at an exposition organized in 1974 in Spokane, Washington, a city only one-third the size of Seattle and one-fifth the size of San Antonio. This fair attempted to accomplish the same purposes as did the fairs of the two larger cities: to stimulate physical and economic renewal in a stagnant center city area and to celebrate an uplifting contemporary social issue. To those ends Spokane's civic leaders added another purpose: to convince the public that an ecological theme could be developed for the fair that would promote the revitalization of downtown Spokane.

That ambitious plan originated in the early 1960s with the realization by Spokane city officials that the economic health of their downtown was threatened by the growth of suburban shopping centers. To respond to that threat, Spokane Unlimited, a downtown planning organization, was created, and it hired Ebasco Services, a consulting firm from New York City, to draw up a master plan. Finished in 1961, that plan called for a large pedestrian mall, a renovated riverfront, and a government building complex in an open, grassy zone. But in 1962 and again in 1964, voters rejected a $10.5 million bond issue to implement the plan.

About that time interest in celebrating Spokane's centennial developed. A Los Angeles firm, Economic Research Associates, was hired to assess the feasibility of combining some kind of exhibition with the centennial and concluded that a regional celebration would not yield enough money to complete needed civic improvements. The consultants suggested, however, that a world's fair, based on the theme of ecology, would be the best way to reclaim downtown Spokane. King Cole, an urban expert who headed an organization called Association for a Better Community (ABC), was enthusiastic, and by the late 1960s planning for a fair began. The date was set for 1974, one of three possible centennial dates, because there was not enough time to hold a fair earlier, and holding it later would conflict with the national bicentennial celebration of American independence. After voters rejected yet another bond issue, civic leaders persuaded the business community to accept a business and occupation tax to raise capital for the fair.[27]

The most desirable site for Expo '74 lay along the Spokane River, but most of that land was owned by three railroads. After months of negotiation, fair officials convinced the railroads to donate the land for the fair site. In Washington, D.C., Sen. Warren G. Magnuson once again used his considerable influence to obtain federal subsidies for a fair in his home state, including an $11.5 million appropriation for a federal government pavilion. Effective lobbying before the state legislature resulted in $10.5 million in state funds for the fair. As plans progressed, Spokane leaders had trouble attracting corporate exhibitors. Lee Iacocca of Ford summed up the feelings of many when he said, "Where the hell's Spokane?" The fair's organizers made major efforts to bring potential exhibitors to Spokane and to sell them on the fair by showing them the city and the site. At the same time a thaw in international affairs highlighted by a summit meeting between President Richard Nixon and Soviet Premier Leonid Brezhnev led to a commitment from the U.S.S.R. to participate. That promise lent credibility to the entire exposition and encouraged other nations (and some corporations) to come to Spokane.[28]

President Nixon opened Expo '74 on May 4. Although he was mired in the Watergate scandal that would drive him from office in just three months, the president spoke grandly about how the fair could create a new environment of world peace: "Let this be a day in which we concentrate, and consecrate as well, not only our efforts in America but also working with peoples in other nations toward the goal of a fresh new environment in terms of peace for all mankind." Visitors could see exhibits from nine foreign nations, seven northwestern states and Canadian provinces, sixty-two corporations, and twenty-six special category entities, such as an African American display and one sponsored by the Washington State Wheat Commission. An amusement area, known as Universa, contained twenty-one rides. One ride, called Ride Over the Falls, transported fair-goers over the foamy, roaring wonder of the mighty Spokane Falls, which, in the absence of a tower or other similar structure, became the centerpiece of the fair. Four different entertainment venues presented a wide variety of musical and theatrical artists. On the whole critics approved of the fair. Dave Holstrom, a reporter for the *Christian Science Monitor*, wrote that "the fair is very attractive. Although it's not as big as the New York fair, for example, it's a pocket sized exposition that's on a good human scale. One expert fair watcher here remarked that it's the only fair which has taken its theme structure from a natural feature—the Spokane River and falls. And it's the only one with a natural phenomenon—the river—going through the grounds. The others had artificial structures for the theme, such as the Space Needle."[29]

Both the U.S. and the Soviet Pavilions, the most popular at the fair, emphasized the ecology theme of the fair, "Celebrating Tomorrow's Fresh, New Environment." While the Soviet Pavilion leaned heavily toward scientific presentations in film and static exhibits, the U.S. Pavilion featured

Environmental issues formed the theme of Expo '74. The U.S. Pavilion, shown here, raised the consciousness of visitors about the environment. (Expo '74 press kit photo by Walter Hodges, courtesy of John E. Findling)

an IMAX film about the environment and a one-acre garden courtyard with exhibits about the relationship of the environment to everyday life. Near the fairgrounds a series of symposia on ecological topics lent substance to the fair's theme. The United Nations designated the fair as the focal point of World Environment Day activities on June 5. Reflecting the success of the civil rights movement of the 1960s, the $500,000 African American Pavilion featured the work of black artists, musicians, and writers. Visitors were led around by guides in colorful dashikis, and politics was never an issue. For their part women had no pavilion at Expo '74, but a woman's day was held, at which speakers praised Washington State's recent ratification of the Equal Rights Amendment. Later a three-day conference on "Women and the Environment" was held under the fair's auspices at nearby Gonzaga University.[30]

The fair closed on November 4 with total attendance at 5.6 million, some 1.5 million more than the number estimated to allow the fair to break even financially. Spokane was true to the fair's theme by building a state-of-the-art sewage treatment plant that did much to clean up the Spokane River. In addition the fair inspired new buildings in downtown Spokane, including a skywalk system, a hotel, two bank towers, and a large department store. Other older buildings were renovated. In 1976 the fair site reopened as Riverfront Park, a popular amusement center.[31]

As early as 1962, there was talk of a great world's fair to mark the bicentennial of the United States in 1976. Seen as a natural successor to the fairs in Philadelphia in 1876 and 1926, a bicentennial exposition might bring further civic improvements to Philadelphia and make that city the center of all bicentennial activities. That was the thinking of a Philadelphia citizens' group that was formed in 1962 and worked on planning such an exposition during the rest of the decade. Problems developed in the early 1970s when Philadelphia Mayor Frank Rizzo announced his opposition to the site and to the idea of a large exposition in general. By that time, too, the American Revolution Bicentennial Commission (ARBC), formed in 1966 to coordinate all bicentennial observances, concluded that it would not support a large international exposition because of the cost, the lack of preparation time, and the belief that poor people would not be able to afford the price of admission. The ARBC suggested that a national bicentennial celebration consisting of many smaller events be developed, and the Philadelphia committee dropped its plans for a 1976 world's fair.[32]

The relative success of the fairs in San Antonio and Spokane, combined with the failure of plans for a major exposition in Philadelphia, set a pattern for the immediate future. World's fairs, it seemed, would be held in smaller cities. In the 1980s fairs were held in Knoxville and New Orleans, but unanticipated difficulties with both deterred other cities, notably Chicago, from hosting fairs, and the New Orleans fair of 1984 was the last twentieth-century fair in the United States.

The Spokane fair, Expo '74, was the inspiration for the Knoxville International Energy Exposition of 1982. Stewart Evans, the executive director of the Downtown Knoxville Association, attended Expo '74 and thought Knoxville, a city similar in size to Spokane, could do the same. There was little enthusiasm at first, but gradually civic leaders, including Jacob F. "Jake" Butcher, president of the United America Bank, began to support the idea as a way to benefit the city and, not so coincidentally, themselves. The city council endorsed the idea of an exposition and moved forward with planning, ignoring requests from a sizable opposition organization that a public referendum be held with respect to putting on the fair. Meanwhile Butcher's ties with President Jimmy Carter and, especially, his budget director, Atlanta banker Bert Lance, were useful in obtaining federal support for the fair.[33]

The exposition's site was a sixty-five-acre plot not far from downtown known as Lower Second Creek, a stream running the length of the city, partly in a tunnel. The proposed site had little public access and a railroad track running through it. Exposition planners thought the stream and the rest of the site could be cleaned up and made useful. By the time of the fair, the stream had been buried and a shallow four-acre pond, called Waters of the World, had been constructed, but the railroad track proved too expensive to move and remained in place throughout the fair. Pedestrian bridges over the track allowed visitors to get from one side of the fairgrounds to the other.

The theme of the exposition, contrived in the context of the energy crisis of the mid-1970s, was Energy Turns the World, and it seemed fitting inasmuch as Knoxville was the home of the Tennessee Valley Authority, a regional energy system built during the 1930s. In addition Knoxville lies near Oak Ridge, the site of the National Atomic Energy Laboratory, and is not far from the coal deposits in the Cumberland Mountains. Exhibits from twenty-four nations, thirty corporations, and seven states generally reflected the theme, although it could best be seen in the $21.1 million U.S. Pavilion, which included an IMAX film on America's energy resources and numerous exhibits on energy availability and use in the United States. An interactive video system allowed visitors to express their opinions about energy issues, and other video displays informed visitors about different forms of energy production. Most of the international participants hewed to the energy theme as well in their pavilions, although Egypt, Peru, and China all displayed historical relics, and Hungary's exhibit focused on the then popular Rubik's Cube, developed by Hungarian mathematician Erno Rubik.

The fair's architecture incorporated several older buildings on the site, much as had been done in San Antonio, and blended them with the large cantilevered U.S. Pavilion and the 266-foot Sunsphere, the fair's signature structure. Because the BIE regulations required that as hosts of a category

Professor Erno Rubik, holding his cube, sits with Jay Brandon, winner of the Rubik's Cube competition, outside the Hungarian pavilion at the Knoxville International Energy Exposition. (Photo courtesy of Cyndy B. Waters)

II or theme fair the Knoxville organizers had to provide exhibit space for international and corporate exhibitors, many of the fair's other structures were prefabricated modular buildings of the kind seen at San Antonio and Spokane.

The Knoxville fair succeeded in many respects. It met its attendance projection of eleven million visitors and broke even financially, partly due to the new technique of selling sponsorships to large corporations, entitling their products to be the "official" product of the fair. Thus, for example, Coca-Cola was the official soft drink, Popeye Popcorn was the official popcorn, Gerber was the official baby food, and Cimarron Carpets were the official carpets of the Knoxville fair. The fair enjoyed success on another level as well: ideological. It helped to alleviate concerns about the energy crisis by promising abundant energy for American domestic consumption far into the future. The global environmental crisis had been brought under control, or so it seemed at the fair, and Americans could relax and entrust the fate of the planet to the corporations that provided abundant energy for an abundant style of living.[34]

The glistening Sunsphere at the Knoxville International Energy Exposition represented a new interest in solar energy. (Photo courtesy of Cyndy B. Waters)

The reputation and legacy of the Knoxville fair have been inextricably linked with the collapse of the Butcher banking empire just months after the fair closed. Jake Butcher, the chairman of the fair board, had developed a reputation in the 1970s as a hard-driving, aggressive banker. By the early 1980s he had amassed a considerable fortune and had run twice for governor of Tennessee, losing each time. In February 1983 the United America Bank, Butcher's flagship bank, closed; its losses were estimated at $15 million. It was the third largest bank failure in American banking history. In May five more Butcher-controlled banks closed, and later in the year Butcher had to sell his interests in yet other banks to avoid personal bankruptcy. Meanwhile federal and state authorities were investigating the banking practices of Butcher, his brother C. H. Butcher Jr., and other associates, and in November Jake Butcher was indicted on numerous counts of fraud. A plea bargain agreement was reached in April, and in June 1985 Butcher was sentenced to two concurrent twenty-year prison terms, while he was still under investigation for other crimes in Memphis, as well as in Kentucky and Florida. Because the fair's money was tied up in Butcher's banks, any surplus was lost, and plans for the future development of the fair site were never carried out.

In February 1984 the federal government sold the U.S. Pavilion to Knoxville for $1.00, having been unable to find any other suitable buyer. The city planned to convert the pavilion into a science and technology museum, but those plans were never implemented, and the pavilion was demolished in 1988. The Sunsphere and its revolving restaurant operated for a time after the fair, but the restaurant failed, and the tower was closed. In the mid-1990s, its observation deck was reopened to tourists.[35]

If the Knoxville fair gained a reputation as having been a disaster only after it closed, the Louisiana World Exposition in New Orleans in 1984 had the reputation as being a disaster from start to finish. The idea for this fair originated in October 1974 with a suggestion by Edward Stagg, the executive director of the Council for a Better Louisiana, that a fair be held in 1980; that idea was endorsed by the Louisiana Tourist Development Commission. In December 1975 Gov. Edwin Edwards appointed a planning committee. After Ewen Dingwall, the general manager of the Century 21 Exposition in Seattle, produced a positive feasibility study, the state created the Louisiana Exposition Authority to represent the state in exposition matters. New Or-

Much of the decoration that graced the Wonderwall at the Louisiana World Exposition in 1984 was derived from Mardi Gras float figures. (Photo courtesy of Jerry Uliano)

leans Mayor Ernest N. Morial likewise endorsed the idea of a fair but demanded that the fair's managers reimburse the city for expenses related to its site development.

By 1977 the date of the fair had been pushed back to 1984, and in 1979 the BIE sanctioned the New Orleans fair, contingent on satisfactory funding. By 1981 organizers claimed to have $37.5 million in pledges and a lease on an eighty-one-acre site along the Mississippi River. International and corporate participation came slowly, however. When the fair opened, about twenty foreign nations and a similar number of corporations were represented, many in collective exhibits. Probably many corporations chose to involve themselves in the 1984 Summer Olympic Games in Los Angeles rather than to help sponsor the New Orleans fair.[36]

The theme of the fair was the World of Rivers: Fresh Water as a Source of Life, and many exhibits focused on that theme. The U.S. Pavilion, for example, showed visitors a 70mm, three-dimensional film titled *Water: The Source of Life*, which took viewers to many water-related sites around the country. The pavilion also had extensive displays of water applications, including fusion power, and water habitats of plants and animals. The New Orleans fair had no signature structure, such as a tower; instead, fair architects made their statement with the Wonderwall, a complex, multistory midway that was twenty-six hundred feet long, included all kinds of architectural motifs, and contained a wide variety of shops, outdoor stages, and food stands. Conceived by California architects Charles Moore and William Turnbull in collaboration with local architects Arthur Anderson and Leonard Salvato, the Wonderwall was originally intended to be a dividing point between the modern architecture of some of the exposition zones, or neighborhoods, and an area of renovated older warehouses, but it grew beyond its original purpose to become the central feature at the fair. Although the Wonderwall was criticized by many architects and writers, it was popular with visitors. The fair also included a monorail system suspended between two 356-foot towers. The site was divided into six neighborhoods, all but one flanking the Wonderwall. The International Riverfront featured the U.S. and foreign pavilions, the Bayou Plaza included some corporate exhibits, and the Great Hall included a large auditorium called the Great Hall, as well as the Louisiana Pavilion, the African American Pavilion, with exhibits reflecting the black experience in America, and the women's pavilion, a geodesic dome with art by American women and a photographic exhibit showing a century of women's contributions. Other neighborhoods included the Centennial Plaza, which was highlighted by the Centennial Pavilion that reflected the architecture and ambience of the 1884–85 New Orleans World's Industrial and Cotton Centennial Exposition, as well as exhibits by the oil and electrical industries. Fulton Mall showcased the Vatican and city of New Orleans pavilions, and, finally, Festival Park, the fair's midway, featured an Italian Village and various rides.

As had been the case at Spokane, the African American Pavilion at the New Orleans fair was dedicated to celebrating the artistic achievements of blacks. Designed by John Scott, a local artist, the twelve hundred square foot pavilion, called "I've Known Rivers, Inc.," contained colorful obelisks of African inspiration, photographic murals, and other kinds of audiovisual

The whimsical Wonderwall provided the crowds with a wealth of entertainment and food choices. (Photo courtesy of Jerry Uliano)

presentations of the black experience in America, as well as music, dance, and lecture programs. After the fair closed, the pavilion became a museum and cultural center. The women's pavilion focused more on history, informing visitors about the gains women had made in American society since the first New Orleans fair a century before.[37]

Because of construction cost overruns, slow advance ticket sales, and the lack of corporate sponsors, the fair's financial problems were apparent even before opening day. But the fair opened on schedule, hosting a crowd disappointed by President Ronald Reagan's last-minute decision not to attend the opening ceremonies. From the beginning attendance lagged behind predictions and was hurt still more by negative reports regarding unfinished pavilions and attractions.[38]

Attendance for the six months of the fair totaled 7.2 million, less than half the projected total, and the financial picture quickly turned from bad to worse. In August the fair was unable to make its tax payments. Then, on October 2, Governor Edwards termed the fair a "disaster," noting that "if this had been a public venture, there would have been people sent to the state penitentiary." A number of the fair's top officials were fired within the next few days, and on October 5 the former marketing director, Frank Kennedy, was indicted for engaging in a kickback scheme wherein he received payments from companies that his office licensed to sell souvenir items at the fair. In early November, just six days before the fair closed, the fair board filed for bankruptcy, listing debts of $121 million. Late that month court officials halted demolition of the fair's structures until it could be determined whether any could be sold as a means of reducing the fair's indebtedness. A three-day auction was held in early January 1985, but that effort raised comparatively little money. The U.S. Pavilion, for example, was sold for $130,000 to a Boston export agent who had no idea what he would do with it. The pavilion had cost $5.5 million to build. Whatever money was raised at the auction was turned over to the Federal Bankruptcy Court and used to pay some of the 750 creditors who had filed claims amounting to $81 million. Litigation regarding the financial problems of the New Orleans fair continued for many years.[39]

What went wrong? There were no clear-cut answers. Petr Spurney, the general manager of the New Orleans fair and a veteran exposition administrator, said, "Fairs have to create a once-in-a-lifetime experience" for visitors and admitted that that challenge was the most serious he and his staff had confronted. John D. Kramer, then involved in planning for the proposed 1992 fair in Chicago, thought that the New Orleans fair was too close in time and place to Knoxville; it was simply the wrong kind of fair in the wrong city at the wrong time. But King Cole, president of the Spokane fair board and a consultant to the 1992 Chicago fair, said that the financial problems of New Orleans did not necessarily mean the fair was a failure; perhaps that is the wrong standard by which to judge a fair. One had to consider the residuals, such as renovating or sprucing up an area or improving a city's image. The civic leaders of New Orleans hoped to capitalize on that idea by holding a Riverfront Awareness Week on the first anniversary of the exposition's opening. It was noted at public meetings and in the press that the fair had left a $93 million convention center, $60 million in street and sidewalk improvements, a $55 million new retail complex, and eight thousand new hotel rooms. A conference was held to discuss ways to continue building on that legacy, but many were skeptical, feeling that the improvements would have come without the fair.

As it turned out, even the residuals did not look very good. In 1985 hoteliers were complaining about a sharp drop in occupancy rates, and by 1986 the city, which had lost $2.8 million on the fair, was in financial straits to such an extent that city offices were closed on Fridays to save money. Perhaps the most significant legacy of the New Orleans fair was the death blow it dealt to the 1992 Chicago exposition.[40]

The quincentennial of Columbus's landfall in America came in 1992, and as early as 1977 the idea that Chicago should celebrate that event with a world's fair had surfaced. Harry Weese, a Chicago architect, first suggested a 1992 fair that would also commemorate the centennial of the World's Columbian Exposition. In 1981 a number of fair boosters, headed by Thomas Ayers, a utility company executive, created a private organization, Chicago World's Fair 1992 Corporation. Within a year that group had planned a theme, set dates for the fair, located a site along Lake Michigan just north of the Century of Progress site, and applied to the BIE for sanction.

Opposition to the fair developed in 1982 and 1983 around the secretive nature of Ayers's group, which some believed was developing the fair in a self-serving manner, and the feeling that significant issues, such as financing and the environmental impact of the fair, were not being sufficiently considered. Some thought the site plan, drawn up by the noted architectural firm of Skidmore, Owings, and Merrill, was unworkable. The site would include 160 acres of new landfill, with no residual facilities. One critic compared it with a nuclear airplane: "too costly to build, too big to fly." State and local officials intervened, and in late 1983 they created a new committee, Chicago World's Fair 1992 Authority, to replace the private committee.[41]

A serious blow to the fair's chances for success came in April 1983 with Harold Washington's election as the first black American to serve as Chicago's mayor. Washington had expressed only lukewarm support for the fair and was skeptical about the amount of public funding such a large enterprise would require, not only for building the fair itself, but also for the improvements in streets, sidewalks, sewers, and the like that would be needed to accommodate the fair and the expected crowds of visitors. Many of Washington's political supporters, moreover, argued that long-neglected black and Hispanic neighborhoods needed public funds far more than did a large, showy, and temporary world's fair.[42]

Dissension first surfaced in December 1983 at the first meeting of the

Chicago World's Fair 1992 Authority, when sharp division was evident between business leaders, who supported the fair for the economic benefits they thought it would bring to the city (and to their businesses), and minority representatives, who saw little of usefulness to their constituencies in a fair. A heated political debate over the fair continued throughout 1984 and into 1985, during which time considerable attention was paid to the debacle of the New Orleans fair. Public support for the undertaking dwindled, and no consensus was ever achieved concerning the fair and what it might mean for the city and its people.

While city leaders debated the merits of the fair, the state legislature also considered the issue of state funding for an event that many felt would benefit only the Chicago area. In the early months of 1985, pro-fair supporters worried that the New Orleans experience would make it much harder to obtain needed state funding for their fair, and their worries were justified. Many downstate legislators were also concerned about the lack of consensus within Chicago about what the fair's impact was to be, where it would be located, and how it should be financed. The state legislature authorized a feasibility study, which recommended that no state funds go to a Chicago fair because such a fair might well lose as much as $350 million. With that, and with the fresh memories of New Orleans, state legislative leaders withdrew their support. Without state money, the fair could never be staged, and while some residual interest remained in putting together a smaller, privately funded event, the idea for a great international exposition was dead in the water by the end of 1985.[43]

In a perceptive article written in 1965, "Goodbye to World's Fairs," Russell Lynes criticized many aspects of the ongoing New York World's Fair and noted that internationalism might be the reason why great fairs are doomed. In the late nineteenth and early twentieth centuries, visitors could go to fairs and literally see the wonders of the world; attending a world's fair was a fantasy substitute for travel. By the 1960s the world's marvels could be bought in stores, seen on television, and admired in museums. Twenty years later, Mike Royko, a *Chicago Tribune* columnist, echoed the same sentiments in an article about the demise of the 1992 Chicago world's fair. Royko wrote that one reason the Chicago fair failed to materialize was that no one in Chicago really got very excited about it because fairs were no longer special or magical as they had been in 1893 or 1933–34, when the city had hosted its earlier world's fairs.[44]

Since the collapse of plans for the 1992 Chicago world's fair, few American cities have seriously considered staging a world's fair, although world's fairs are still put on successfully in other countries. Fairs in Brisbane, Australia (1988), Seville, Spain (1992), Taejon, South Korea (1993), and Lisbon, Portugal (1998) were all successful events, and expectations for the turn-of-the-century fair in Hannover, Germany, in 2000 are very high. Whether the success of those fairs will encourage entrepreneurs and promoters in the United States to celebrate the twenty-first century with a new round of American fairs remains to be seen.

CONCLUSION

Cultural Dinosaurs? World's Fairs and the Survival of the Species

*S*ince the middle of the nineteenth century, world's fairs have been marching across and leaving lasting imprints on the landscape of the modern world. We sometimes think that fairs are cultural dinosaurs, that they have been displaced by theme parks, Olympic spectacles, and electronically mediated forms of education and entertainment that range from virtual universities to pornographic websites—antecedents of which can be found in the web of world's fairs that have ringed the globe beginning with London's 1851 Crystal Palace Exhibition. But world's fairs show no sign of becoming extinct. A major world's fair concluded in Seville in 1992; another took place in Lisbon in 1998. Hannover is hosting a major universal exposition in 2000, and plans are also under way for the Aichi World Expo 2005 near Nagoya, Japan. The pace of world's fair building may have slackened since the turn of the last century when international expositions were held every year, but world's fairs continue to be held. More to the point, they continue to provide us with ideological and cultural armor that is analogous to the armor that some dinosaurs once evolved to ensure their survival. The real question is not whether world's fairs have become cultural dinosaurs. The real question is whether the armor with which they have outfitted the modern world will enable us to survive as a species for anything like the length of time that dinosaurs walked the earth.[1]

From their inception in 1851, world's fairs have mirrored the rise of the modern industrial nation-states and reflected their specific national imperial policies. With their spectacular technological and ethnological narratives, fairs engaged in the mission of "manufacturing consent."[2] Cultural sociologist Tony Bennett has aptly described that process:

> To identify with power, to see it as, if not directly theirs, then indirectly so, a force regulated and channelled by society's ruling groups but for the good of all: this was the rhetoric of power embodied in the exhibitionary complex—a power made manifest not in its ability to inflict pain but by its ability to organize and co-ordinate an order of things and to produce a place for the people in relation to that order.[3]

Why was it so imperative for world's fair sponsors to win over the hearts and minds of their national publics? The alternative, in the eyes of the ruling elites who organized world's fairs between 1876 and 1916, was social and political revolution.

In Europe political upheavals continued after the 1848 revolutions. In 1871 the Paris Commune sent shock waves around the continent and across the Atlantic Ocean. Then in 1917 capitalists around the world awoke to a full-fledged communist revolution in Russia. The United States was hardly immune to class violence that resulted from its own breakneck pace of industrialization. In 1873, in the midst of efforts to reconstruct the nation after the Civil War, a financial panic precipitated the first in a series of post–Civil War industrial depressions. The upsurge of political radicalism and industrial violence in the 1880s and 1890s made many Americans wonder if the war between the North and the South had been only a prelude to a war that would pit one social class against another.

If the prospects of social and political revolution posed threats to nation-building projects in the United States and Europe in the late nineteenth and early twentieth centuries, the threat to national order seemed even greater from the worldwide collapse of capitalism between the world wars. As they had done before World War I, ruling national elites once again turned to the medium of the world's fair to win over the hearts and minds of both national and colonial populations to the rightness and naturalness of ruling class authority. The 1920s and 1930s witnessed an upsurge in colonial expositions in Europe that were intended to maintain public support for specific national imperial policies. In the United States the emphasis was on neoimperialism, building support for U.S. economic involvement and, if necessary, military intervention in foreign countries deemed vital to America's industrial and agricultural growth.

During the cold war, world's fairs continued to be ideologically scored but in a different key. The goal in Europe and the United States was to win popular support for the crusade against communism and to promote the globalization of corporate capitalism.

Once the cold war was won, world's fairs began to reflect the growing power of transnational corporate capitalism as a potential rival to the nation-states that, historically, world's fairs had helped call into being. At the 1992 Seville exposition, corporations such as Rank Xerox and Siemens had a commanding presence, both as exhibitors with distinctive pavilions and as underwriters of national exhibits. A century before, at the 1893 Chicago fair, only 9 of the approximately 137 exposition structures had been erected by private businesses. By 1933 twenty major corporations had their own pavilions. Clearly world's fairs, both in the United States and abroad, have served to advance the twin causes of nationalism and capitalism. Now, at the close of the twentieth century, as anthropologist Penelope Harvey has pointed out at the Seville exposition, "we find the harnessing of national identities to corporate ends."[4]

As we survey the history of world's fairs, it is clear that technology has played a crucial role in ideological innovation. For instance, at the very beginning of the world's fair movement with London's Crystal Palace Exhibition, one display in particular spoke volumes about the shape of things to come—the display of Samuel Colt's repeating revolver, which was part of the American exhibit at the fair.

As the story is usually told in histories of technology and industrialization, the American exhibit at the 1851 exhibition, with its guns and reapers, opened the eyes of the British to the accomplishments of their American rivals, who suddenly seemed poised to challenge the industrial superiority of Great Britain. No doubt the British learned from the American exhibit, and no doubt the Crystal Palace Exhibition, like every succeeding fair, served as a technology transfer site. But in the case of Colt's repeating revolver, technical information was only part of the transfer. What was also conveyed was the allegory of imperial conquest.

Witness the account of the Colt revolver display in a U.S. Senate committee report that made its way into the *Official Descriptive and Illustrated Catalogue* of the Crystal Palace:

On the Texan frontier, and on the several routes to California, the Indian tribes are renewing their murderous warfare, and a general Indian war is likely to ensue, unless bodies of mounted men, efficiently equipped for such service, are em-

The Eiffel Tower, which was constructed for the 1889 Paris Universal Exposition, is still that city's most familiar landmark. (Photo courtesy of John E. Findling)

ployed against them. . . . A few bold men, well skilled in the use of [Colt revolvers] can, under such circumstances, encounter and scatter almost any number of savages.

As the *Catalogue* made clear, Colt revolvers became world's fair souvenirs of a special sort. "A considerable number of [the revolvers] have been taken from the Exhibition," the *Catalogue* reported, "and sent for trial in Her Majesty's Service, to the Cape of Good Hope, against the Kafirs."[5] This was a case of technology transfer with a vengeance.

In addition to transferring technologies and allegories of imperial tri-

Pan=American Souvenir Coffee Spoon. Quality Strictly First Grade.

This is a very fine quality souvenir spoon, made especially to order for the Lake Shore & Michigan Southern Railway, by the Oneida Community, at their factory, Niagara Falls, N. Y. It is fully guaranteed by that concern as an EXTRA QUALITY SPOON, and we fully recommend it.

The ornamentation on face and back is very fine. This very beautiful, appropriate and lasting souvenir sent postpaid to any address for twenty (20) cents in coin.

Detach coupon below, fill in your name and address plainly and mail direct to factory. If you do not wish to mutilate magazine, spoon will be sent upon receipt of price, without coupon.

Lake Shore Pan-American Souvenir Coupon.

THE ONEIDA COMMUNITY, Niagara Falls, N. Y.

Enclosed find twenty cents in coin for which send me one L. S. & M. S. Ry. Souvenir Coffee Spoon. Address

Name ....

No. .... Street

City .... State.......

The facilities afforded by the Lake Shore for travel between the west and the Pan American Exposition are unsurpassed, no other line presenting so remarkable a train service or so interesting a route. Its through train service between Chicago and Toledo, Cleveland, Buffalo, New York and Boston, excels all others. "Book of Pan-American" and "Book of Trains" sent free on request.
A. J. SMITH, G. P. & T. A., Cleveland, O.

When you write, please mention "The Cosmopolitan."

From the early days of fairs, businesses found that having an association with a world's fair could be profitable as this advertisement from the September 1901 issue of *Cosmopolitan* magazine illustrates.

umph across national boundaries, world's fairs generated powerful feelings of technological utopianism that shored up sagging public confidence in the capacity of industry and technology to solve social and political problems.[6] Engineering feats like the Eiffel Tower, built for the 1889 Paris Universal Exposition, or the Ferris Wheel, constructed for the 1893 Chicago fair, inspired confidence in many fairgoers in the capacity of world's fair organizers to engineer a better future. With the rapid electrification of world's fairs by the beginning of the twentieth century, who could doubt that the future would be brighter? So rampant was technological utopianism in world's fair discourse that one U.S. senator claimed to be able to see far into the future from the platform he occupied at the 1898 Trans-Mississippi and International Exposition in Omaha:

Miraculous as has been the growth in wealth and numbers of the trans-Mississippi region, its capacities are but imperfectly suspected, even by those who have been boldest in their predictions. It will support a population of 250,000,000 without taxing its resources to exhaustion, and by the close of the twentieth century its possessions will far exceed its assets now inscribed on the national ledger. Science will discover new applications for overcoming obstacles of nature. The inventions of Edison will replenish the treasuries of the world with the gold of its mountain ranges, and the discoveries of Tesla may convert the wasted forces of its winds and rivers into applied energy that will carry on all the operations of industry without the intervention of human labor.[7]

The claim that utopia was nigh, if only people would place their trust in those with the technical and scientific knowledge, not to mention access to the capital resources necessary to bring it about, would remain the mantra of world's fair organizers well into the twentieth century. Sometimes the results of that conviction led to astonishing, futuristic world's fair spectacles; sometimes the results were astonishing plans for spectacles that were never held.

As many scholars have noted, technological utopianism continued to run rampant in the 1930s.[8] Nowhere were its ideological underpinnings better expressed than in the unofficial motto of the 1933–34 Chicago Century of Progress Exposition: "Science Finds; Industry Applies; Man Conforms."[9] That same core sentiment carried forward into the 1939 New York World's Fair where General Motors' Futurama became the hit of the fair. Intended to sell cars and to promote public financing of highways, Futurama was much more. It was a vision of a planned future where technology and science, wedded to corporate capitalism, made social and economic problems seemingly disappear. That vision was so compelling that news of the New York World's Fair heightened the determination of Italian dictator Benito Mussolini to hold his own fascistic world-of-tomorrow exposition— the so-called E-42 fair planned for Rome in 1942. Designed by the major architect of fascist Italy, Macello Piacentini, E-42 never came off because of the war, but several of his exposition palaces were constructed and did survive the war. Like other permanent world's fair buildings (for instance, the main buildings erected for two San Diego world's fairs that now form the core of the museum complex in Balboa Park), several of the E-42 structures became museums, adding additional layers to the cultural armor that world's fairs have evolved to assure, at least in theory, the survival of the human species.[10]

By the 1930s technologies of mass communication and consumption were buttressing the utopian blueprints laid down by world's fair authorities. The 1893 World's Columbian Exposition in Chicago, for instance, boasted a massive public relations operation capable of saturating mass audiences with a variety of print and visual media messages intended to promote tourism and other forms of mass consumption. Furthermore, by the 1930s, display techniques, including new forms of machine-age spectacle developed by industrial designers such as Norman Bel Geddes and Walter Dorwin Teague, brought earlier dream worlds of imperial abundance to life at fairs on both sides of the Atlantic.[11] In the case of American fairs, as Roland Marchand has made clear, entertainment began to surpass education as the overriding feature of pavilions organized by corporations. Indeed, technologies capable of providing entertainment—ranging from thrill rides to technologically sophisticated peep shows—became permanent fixtures of international expositions.[12]

The utopian potential associated with technology and consumerism, so clear at fairs held during the late nineteenth and early twentieth centuries and at the expositions held between the world wars, reached new heights at the 1958 Brussels Universal Exposition, the 1962 Seattle Century 21 Exposition, and the 1964 New York World's Fair. With fears of nuclear annihilation not far from the forefront of most people's minds, organizers of those fairs did their best to allay concerns and to rekindle popular confidence in the ability of science and technology to pave the way to utopia. The Brussels fair featured the towering Atomium to convince people that nuclear energy was an ally, not a foe, while the Seattle exposition featured the soaring Space Needle that hinted at potential avenues of escape into outer space if the pressing contradictions of modern life became too much to bear. Avoiding those contradictions through sheer exertion of the will was the subtext of the New York World's Fair—a New Jerusalem ushered in by robotics and entertainment. Summing up the essence of all of those fairs, the U.S. secretary of commerce put matters succinctly in remarks at the Seattle exposition: "We are not interested in gloom or doom. We are interested in hope and confidence."[13]

Trying to sound upbeat, that high-ranking U.S. government official was not entirely convincing. Five years later a more chastened vision of the future came to light in Montreal at Expo '67 with its questioning subtheme: "Man in Control?"[14] By 1974 Spokane's Expo '74, also called the International Exposition on the Environment, gave visible expression to growing concerns about environmental degradation. That theme would recur at subsequent expositions, usually in contexts that held out the promise of finding technological solutions to economic and political problems rooted in the often horrific consequences that have followed from the globalization of corporate capitalism.

Historically, world's fairs have always proffered technological solutions to

The Atomium at the Brussels Universal Exposition in 1958 was designed to promote the peaceful use of nuclear energy. (Photo courtesy of John E. Findling)

social, economic, and political problems. At the same time world's fairs have themselves been cultural technologies that have nurtured—in rough chronological sequence—nationalism, imperialism, and neoimperialism. Whether world's fairs can literally shed their skins and evolve new ways of addressing the problems that they have helped to create in the first place is an issue that should give pause for thought.

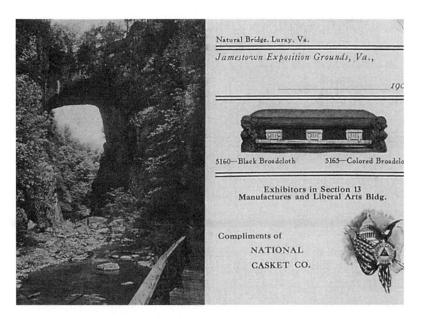

Natural Bridge. Luray. Va.

Jamestown Exposition Grounds, Va.,

190

5160—Black Broadcloth   5165—Colored Broadclo

Exhibitors in Section 13
Manufactures and Liberal Arts Bldg.

Compliments of

NATIONAL

CASKET CO.

From infant incubators to fancy caskets, world's fairs offer something for everyone. (Photo courtesy of John E. Findling)

Some of the early planners of Hannover's Expo 2000 certainly believed they were on the right track. In its impressive précis of the design principles for the Hannover fair, the firm of William McDonough Architects made a surprising, accurate assertion: "We start from the premise that the last several world's fairs have been failures at realistically addressing the historical occasions that gave rise to them."[15] As the designers have envisioned it, Expo 2000 will be "honest about the prospects of future civilization by creating an exemplary place of possibility. But the harsh realities of our global social and ecological crises should not be ignored or hidden behind the smiling veil of corporate or ideological sponsorship. Even the ideology of 'sustainability' must contain criticism of itself and its limitations."[16]

Will Expo 2000 escape the technological utopianism and determinism that has shaped previous fairs? Will it really "be based on ideas of restraint, awareness, and concern for solving the world's problems, not hiding them behind a wall of promising machines," as the authors of the *Hannover Principles* hope?[17] It is too early to tell, of course. But there are reasons for skepticism, especially if one turns to the Expo 2000 website, which proudly proclaims that one component of this fair will treat "The Future as Event." As was the case with its predecessors, this exposition too seems to be headed toward what Umberto Eco has called "hyperreality."[18]

What of the future? With good reason the *Hannover Principles* derived from "fear of a devastated planet." They also reflected a "desire to show that we have a real chance to save [the planet] and continue the evolution of our species at the same time."[19] Clearly the authors of that report have continued to put their faith in the world's fair medium. By insisting on a new ideology of sustainability, as opposed to the older ideology projected by earlier fairs that equated economic and industrial growth and scientific and technological advances with progress, the authors seemed to believe that Hannover's fair could step out of its historically determined skin—one that has functioned primarily to advance the globalization of capitalism—and become something new and positive. We hope they are right. But if the representations of sustainability at the Hannover fair make that ideal contingent upon the globalization of transnational corporate capitalism, there is reason to fear that our culturally produced armor will only get heavier and give us a false sense of security as we lumber toward quagmires as menacing as the La Brea tar pits proved for another species that once inhabited the planet.

NOTES

INTRODUCTION

1. Hubert Howe Bancroft, *The Book of the Fair*, 2 vols. (Chicago: Bancroft Co., 1893); Charles Beard, *A Century of Progress* (New York: Harper & Brothers, 1933); John Mack Faragher, "A Nation Thrown Back upon Itself: Turner and the Frontier," *CultureFront* 2 (Summer 1993): 5–6; Henry Adams, *The Education of Henry Adams* (Boston: Houghton Mifflin Company, 1961).

2. Robert Rydell, *All the World's a Fair: Visions of Empire at American International Expositions, 1876–1916* (Chicago: University of Chicago Press, 1984); and *World of Fairs: The Century-of-Progress Expositions* (Chicago: University of Chicago Press, 1993). Tony Bennett, *The Birth of the Museum* (New York: Routledge, 1995).

3. Keith Walden, *Becoming Modern in Toronto: The Industrial Exhibition and the Shaping of a Late Victorian Culture* (Toronto: University of Toronto Press, 1997); Eric Breitbart, *A World on Display* (Corrales, N.Mex.: New Deal Films, 1994); James Gilbert, *Perfect Cities: Chicago's Utopias of 1893* (Chicago: University of Chicago Press, 1991); Karal Ann Marling, *Blue Ribbon: A Social and Pictorial History of the Minnesota State Fair* (St. Paul, Minn.: Minnesota Historical Society Press, 1990); and Leslie Prosterman, *Ordinary Life, Festival Days* (Washington, D.C.: Smithsonian Institution Press, 1994).

4. Lester G. Moses, *Wild West Shows and the Images of American Indians, 1883–1933* (Albuquerque, N.Mex.: University of New Mexico Press, 1996). There is a growing body of scholarship on women's efforts to control their representations at fairs. The best overview is Mary Frances Cordato, "Representing the Expansion of Woman's Sphere" (Ph.D. diss., New York University, 1989). See also Gail Bederman, *Manliness and Civilization* (Chicago: University of Chicago Press, 1995).

5. Burton Benedict, ed., *The Anthropology of World's Fairs* (London and Berkeley: Scolar Press, 1983). Warren Susman, "Ritual Fairs," *Chicago History* 12 (1983): 14–17.

6. Eric Breitbart, *A World on Display: Photographs from the St. Louis World's Fair 1904* (Albuquerque, N.Mex.: University of New Mexico Press, 1997); Julie K. Brown, *Contesting Images: Photography and the World's Columbian*

Exposition (Tucson, Ariz.: University of Arizona Press, 1994); Eugene Ferguson, *Bibliography of the History of Technology* (Cambridge, Mass.: Society for the History of Technology, 1968); Robert Fox, "Thomas Edison's Parisian Campaign," *Annals of Science* 53 (1996): 157–93; John E. Findling and Kimberly D. Pelle, eds., *Historical Dictionary of World's Fairs and Expositions, 1851–1988* (Westport, Conn.: Greenwood Press, 1990); Neil Harris, *Cultural Excursions: Marketing Appetites and Cultural Tastes in Modern America* (Chicago: University of Chicago Press, 1990); Thomas Hines, *Burnham of Chicago* (New York: Oxford University Press, 1974); David Nye, *American Technological Sublime* (Cambridge, Mass.: MIT Press, 1994); and Brigitte Schroeder-Gudehus and Anne Rasmussen, *Les Fastes du Progrès* (Paris: Flammarion, 1992).

7. John Allwood, *The Great Exhibitions* (London: Cassell and Collier Macmillan, 1977); Alfred Heller, *World's Fairs and the End of Progress* (Corte Madera, Calif.: World's Fair, Inc., 1999); E. L. Doctorow, *World's Fair* (New York: Vintage, 1985); and David Gelernter, *1939: The Lost World of the Fair* (New York: Free Press, 1996).

8. Eric Hobsbawm, *Nations and Nationalism since 1780* (Cambridge: Cambridge University Press, 1992), 191.

1. FAIRS IN THE AGE OF INDUSTRIALISM'S ADVANCE

1. Quoted in Eric de Maré, *London 1851: The Year of the Great Exhibition* (London: Folio Society, 1972), n.p.

2. Patrick Beaver, *The Crystal Palace* (London: Hugh Evelyn Ltd., 1970), 11–19, 23–32.

3. Victoria's diary entry is quoted in de Maré, *London 1851*, n.p. See also Beaver, *The Crystal Palace*, 33–46.

4. Beaver, *The Crystal Palace*, 63–67, 141–47.

5. Ivan Steen, "New York 1853," in *Historical Dictionary of World's Fairs and Expositions, 1851–1988*, ed. John E. Findling and Kimberly D. Pelle (Westport, Conn.: Greenwood Press, 1990), 12.

6. Steen, "New York 1853," 12–13; John Allwood, *The Great Exhibitions* (London: Cassell and Collier Macmillan, 1977), 27–33.

7. Alfred Heller, "Philadelphia 1876," in *Historical Dictionary of World's Fairs and Expositions, 1851–1988*, ed. John E. Findling and Kimberly D. Pelle (Westport, Conn.: Greenwood Press, 1990), 55; Robert W. Rydell, *All the World's a Fair: Visions of Empire at American International Expositions, 1876–1916* (Chicago: University of Chicago Press, 1984), 17–22.

8. Heller, "Philadelphia 1876," 55–58; Rydell, *All the World's a Fair*, 11–17; James L. Dale, *What Ben Beverly Saw at the Great Exposition, by a Chicago Lawyer* (Chicago: Centennial Publishing Co., 1876), 119; William Randel, "John Lewis Reports the Centennial," *Pennsylvania Magazine of History and Biography* 79 (July 1955): 373.

9. Rydell, *All the World's a Fair*, 21–22.

10. Ibid., 22–27.

11. Ibid., 28; Matilda Joslyn Gage, *The Declaration of the Rights of Women: 1876* (Aberdeen, S.Dak.: North Plains Press, 1975), 33–41.
12. Rydell, *All the World's a Fair*, 27–29.
13. Ibid., 36–37; Heller, "Philadelphia 1876," 61.
14. John E. Findling, "Opening the Door to the World: International Expositions in the South, 1881–1907," in *Studies in American Culture*, ed. Dennis Hall, 19, no. 2 (1996): 29–31.
15. Findling, "Opening the Door to the World," 31–32; Rydell, *All the World's a Fair*, 83, 89–93, 97–99.
16. Findling, "Opening the Door to the World," 32–34; Rydell, *All the World's a Fair*, 83–85, 94–97, 101.
17. Findling, "Opening the Door to the World," 34–35; Rydell, *All the World's a Fair*, 80, 85–89, 94–97, 99–100.
18. Findling, "Opening the Door to the World," 35–37.
19. Rydell, *All the World's a Fair*, 97–99.
20. Ibid., 80–89.
21. John E. Findling, *Chicago's Great World's Fairs* (Manchester, England: Manchester University Press, 1994), 7–8; R. Reid Badger, *The Great American Fair: The World's Columbian Exposition and American Culture* (Chicago: N. Hall, 1979), 41–52.
22. Findling, *Chicago's Great World's Fairs*, 8–9; Badger, *The Great American Fair*, 63–66.
23. Rudyard Kipling, *American Notes: Rudyard Kipling's West*, ed. Arrell Morgan Gibson (Norman, Okla.: University of Oklahoma Press, 1981), 139.
24. Donald L. Miller, "The White City," *American Heritage* 44, no. 5 (July–August 1993): 73–75; Findling, *Chicago's Great World's Fairs*, 12–13; Badger, *The Great American Fair*, 31–39.
25. Findling, *Chicago's Great World's Fairs*, 9–15; Badger, *The Great American Fair*, 65–68.
26. Findling, *Chicago's Great World's Fairs*, 15–16; 27–28.
27. Miller, "The White City," 80; Findling, *Chicago's Great World's Fairs*, 16–18; Badger, *The Great American Fair*, 83–85; John T. Rogers, "Authorship of the Pledge of Allegiance to the Flag: A Report," Library of Congress, Legislative Reference Service, 18 July 1957.
28. Findling, *Chicago's Great World's Fairs*, 18, 36–40.
29. Rydell, *All the World's a Fair*, 55–60; Thomas Prasch, "Race and Commerce at the Columbian Exposition," unpublished paper presented at the annual meeting of the Popular Culture Association, Chicago, April 1994. For a thorough treatment of the place of African Americans, women, and nonwhite foreign natives at the World's Columbian Exposition, see Robert W. Rydell, "A Cultural Frankenstein? The Chicago World's Columbian Exposition of 1893," in *Grand Illusions: Chicago's World's Fair of 1893*, ed. Neil Harris et al. (Chicago: Chicago Historical Society, 1993), 141–70.
30. Rydell, "Cultural Frankenstein?," 145–50.
31. Frank A. Cassell, "The Columbian Exposition of 1893 and United States Diplomacy in Latin America," *Mid-America* 67 (October 1985): 110–20.

32. Andrew Carnegie, "Value of the World's Fair to the American People," *The Engineering Magazine* 6, no. 4 (January 1894): 421–22.

33. Raymond L. Wilson, "San Francisco 1894," in *Historical Dictionary of World's Fairs and Expositions, 1851–1988,* ed. John E. Findling and Kimberly D. Pelle (Westport, Conn.: Greenwood Press, 1990), 135–36.

2. FAIRS OF THE IMPERIAL ERA

1. John Hay to Theodore Roosevelt, 27 July 1898, in *The Life and Letters of John Hay,* vol. 2, ed. William Roscoe Thayer (Boston: Houghton Mifflin Company, 1916), 337.

2. Toni Oplt, "Omaha 1898," in *Historical Dictionary of World's Fairs and Expositions, 1851–1988,* ed. John E. Findling and Kimberly D. Pelle (Westport, Conn.: Greenwood Press, 1990), 152; Robert W. Rydell, *All the World's a Fair: Visions of Empire at American International Expositions, 1876–1916* (Chicago: University of Chicago Press, 1984), 108–11; William L. Kahrl, "Omaha United a Nation," *World's Fair* 3, no. 3 (Summer 1983): 4–5.

3. Rydell, *All the World's a Fair,* 113–20; Kahrl, "Omaha United a Nation," 3; Kenneth G. Alfers, "Triumph of the West: The Trans-Mississippi Exposition," *Nebraska History* 53, no. 3 (Fall 1972): 325–26.

4. Rydell, *All the World's a Fair,* 120–25.

5. Lewis L. Gould, "Buffalo 1901," in *Historical Dictionary of World's Fairs and Expositions, 1851–1988,* ed. John E. Findling and Kimberly D. Pelle (Westport, Conn.: Greenwood Press, 1990), 165–68; Rydell, *All the World's a Fair,* 128–30.

6. Rydell, *All the World's a Fair,* 131–36. For a detailed description of the color scheme, see Walter H. Page, "The Pan-American Exposition," *World's Work* 5, no. 2 (August 1901): 1030–38.

7. Rydell, *All the World's a Fair,* 139–44.

8. Gould, "Buffalo 1901," 168; Rydell, *All the World's a Fair,* 137–44; Julian Hawthorne, "Novelties at Buffalo Fair," *The Cosmopolitan* 31, no. 5 (September 1901): 489–92; Robert Grant, "Notes on the Pan-American Exposition," *The Cosmopolitan* 31, no. 5 (September 1901): 460; Richard H. Barry, *Snap Shots on the Midway of the Pan-Am Expo* (Buffalo, N.Y.: R. A. Reid, 1901), 23–30, 37–41, 50–52.

9. Rydell, *All the World's a Fair,* 151–53.

10. Yvonne Condon, "St. Louis 1904," in *Historical Dictionary of World's Fairs and Expositions, 1851–1988,* ed. John E. Findling and Kimberly D. Pelle (Westport, Conn.: Greenwood Press, 1990), 178–81; Rydell, *All the World's a Fair,* 157.

11. Condon, "St. Louis 1904," 183–84; Martha R. Clevenger, ed., *Indescribably Grand: Diaries and Letters from the 1904 World's Fair* (St. Louis, Mo.: Missouri Historical Society Press, 1996), 8, 134, 138.

12. The phrase "white man's burden," taken from a poem of the same name by the British writer Rudyard Kipling, asserted that members of the superior Anglo-Saxon race had a Christian obligation to guide lesser races up the path of civilization.

13. Condon, "St. Louis 1904," 183; Rydell, *All the World's a Fair*, 160–67.

14. Rydell, *All the World's a Fair*, 167–70.

15. Ibid., 170–78.

16. Ibid., 178–82; Clevenger, *Indescribably Grand*, 143.

17. John E. Findling, "World's Fairs and the Olympic Games," *World's Fair* 10, no. 4 (October–December 1990): 13–15.

18. Condon, "St. Louis 1904," 185.

19. Carl Abbott, "Portland 1905," in *Historical Dictionary of World's Fairs and Expositions, 1851–1988*, ed. John E. Findling and Kimberly D. Pelle (Westport, Conn.: Greenwood Press, 1990), 189–90; Robert W. Rydell, "Visions of Empire: International Expositions in Portland and Seattle, 1905–1909," *Pacific Historical Review* 52, no. 1 (February 1983): 38–42.

20. Carl Abbott, *The Great Extravaganza: Portland and the Lewis and Clark Exposition* (Portland: Oregon Historical Society, 1981), 13–24.

21. Rydell, *All the World's a Fair*, 193–97.

22. Abbott, *Great Extravaganza*, 54, 63–64, 71–76; Rydell, "Visions of Empire," 53–56, 63–64.

23. Rydell, *All the World's a Fair*, 193–94.

24. Ibid., 197–203.

25. Raymond L. Wilson, "Seattle 1909," in *Historical Dictionary of World's Fairs and Expositions, 1851–1988*, ed. John E. Findling and Kimberly D. Pelle (Westport, Conn.: Greenwood Press, 1990), 206–7.

26. Burton Benedict, "San Francisco 1915," in *Historical Dictionary of World's Fairs and Expositions, 1851–1988*, ed. John E. Findling and Kimberly D. Pelle (Westport, Conn.: Greenwood Press, 1990), 219–21; Rydell, *All the World's a Fair*, 214–17. For longer discussions of the background and architecture of the PPIE, see Marjorie M. Dobkin, "A Twenty-Five Million Dollar Mirage," in *The Anthropology of World's Fairs*, ed. Burton Benedict (London and Berkeley: Scolar Press, 1983), 66–93; and Gray Brechin, "Sailing to Byzantium: The Architecture of the Fair," in *The Anthropology of World's Fairs*, ed. Burton Benedict (London and Berkeley: Scolar Press, 1983), 94–113.

27. Benedict, "San Francisco 1915," 223–24. See also Elizabeth N. Armstrong, "Hercules and the Muses: Public Art and the Fair," in *The Anthropology of World's Fairs*, ed. Burton Benedict (London and Berkeley: Scolar Press, 1983), 114–33; "Beachy Killed in a Taube Drop," *New York Times*, 15 March 1915.

28. Rydell, *All the World's a Fair*, 218–25.

29. Ibid., 227–29; Benedict, "San Francisco 1915," 225; Alfred Heller, *World's Fairs and the End of Progress* (Corte Madera, Calif.: World's Fair, Inc., 1999), 69–73. Heller questions the assertion that Stella's belly moved by mechanical means and suggests that it may have been just a trompe l'oeil.

30. Benedict, "San Francisco 1915," 225. For a more detailed discussion of the legacy of the fair, see George Starr, "Truth Unveiled: The Fair and Its Interpreters," in *The Anthropology of World's Fairs*, ed. Burton Benedict (London and Berkeley: Scolar Press, 1983), 134–75.

31. Raymond Starr, "San Diego 1915–1916," in *Historical Dictionary of World's Fairs and Expositions, 1851–1988*, ed. John E. Findling and Kimberly D. Pelle (Westport, Conn.: Greenwood Press, 1990), 227.

145

32. Starr, "San Diego 1915–1916," 227–28; *The Official Guide Book of the Panama California Exposition* (San Diego: National Views Co., 1915), 8–9.

33. Rydell, *All the World's a Fair,* 220–23.

34. Ibid., 229–31; *Official Guide Book,* 12–15, 39.

3. FAIRS BETWEEN THE WORLD WARS

1. Committee of One Hundred minutes, Sesqui-Centennial International Exposition, Philadelphia City Archives (PCA), RG 232-1-1; David Glassberg, "Philadelphia 1926," in *Historical Dictionary of World's Fairs and Expositions, 1851–1988,* ed. John E. Findling and Kimberly D. Pelle (Westport, Conn.: Greenwood Press, 1990), 246–47.

2. "Sesquicentennial Opens as Sun Shines," *New York Times,* 1 June 1926; "Gates of Sesqui Thrown Open to World," *Philadelphia Inquirer,* 1 June 1926.

3. "Sesqui Buildings Have Few Exhibits," *Philadelphia Evening Bulletin,* 4 June 1926.

4. Special Events file, Sesqui-Centennial International Exposition, PCA, RG 232-4-5.5; "Philadelphia Mayor Bans Dempsey-Wills Bout in Stadium, but Allows It Elsewhere in City," *New York Times,* 2 March 1926.

5. Women's Department file, Sesqui-Centennial International Exposition, PCA, RG 232-4-11. Both the Henry Ford Museum and Greenfield Village in Michigan and the Mystic Seaport Museum in Connecticut were opened in 1929, probably as a result of the attractiveness of High Street.

6. Glassberg, "Philadelphia 1926," 247–48.

7. "Philadelphia Exposition a Failure," *New York Times,* 8 October 1926; "Philadelphia Fair Never Had a Chance," *New York Times,* 9 October 1926; "Sesquicentennial Fair Comes to an End," *New York Times,* 1 December 1926; "4,622,211 Persons Paid to See Fair," *New York Times,* 2 December 1926.

8. Kay Briegel, "Long Beach 1928," in *Historical Dictionary of World's Fairs and Expositions, 1851–1988,* ed. John E. Findling and Kimberly D. Pelle (Westport, Conn.: Greenwood Press, 1990), 250–51.

9. John E. Findling, *Chicago's Great World's Fairs,* (Manchester, England: Manchester University Press, 1994), 43–49.

10. Ibid., 60–66.

11. Douglas Haskell, "Mixed Metaphors at Chicago," *Architectural Review* 74 (August 1933): 47–48. Visitors' comments are noted in Susan Talbot-Stanaway, "The Giant Jewel," *Chicago History* 22, no. 2 (July 1993): 4–23.

12. Susan Talbot-Stanaway, "The Giant Jewel," 15–19; Findling, *Chicago's Great World's Fairs,* 83–90.

13. Findling, *Chicago's Great World's Fairs,* 67–68, 79, 87.

14. Ibid., 99–111; "Super-Feature Exhibits," (New York: Messmore and Damon, 1938), passim. The official guide to the Century of Progress locates the mechanical cow in the Dairy Building, not the International Harvester Building. See *Official Guide Book of the Fair* (Chicago: A Century of Progress, 1933), 76–77.

15. Findling, *Chicago's Great World's Fairs,* 118–19, 124–26.

16. Robert W. Rydell, *World of Fairs: The Century-of-Progress Expositions*

(Chicago: University of Chicago Press, 1993), 165–71; Findling, *Chicago's Great World's Fairs*, 112–13, 127–28.

17. Findling, *Chicago's Great World's Fairs*, 126–31, 133–37.
18. "Business and 'The Fair,'" *Fortune* 7, no. 5 (31 May 1933): 11–14; Findling, *Chicago's Great World's Fairs*, 145–47; Talbot-Stanaway, "The Giant Jewel," 5.
19. Raymond Starr, "San Diego 1935," in *Historical Dictionary of World's Fairs and Expositions, 1851–1988*, ed. John E. Findling and Kimberly D. Pelle (Westport, Conn.: Greenwood Press, 1990), 278; *San Diego Sun*, special exposition edition, n.d.
20. Starr, "San Diego 1935," 278–79; Walter D. Teague, "Ringing Down the Facts," *Commercial Art* 19 (November 1935): 183–87.
21. Rydell, *World of Fairs*, 171; "Texas Centennial Faces Dispute over Art in Nude," *New York Times*, 6 April 1936; "Great Exposition Opened in Texas," *New York Times*, 7 June 1936.
22. Rydell, *World of Fairs*, 172–81.
23. John E. Vacha, "Biggest Bash: Cleveland's Great Lakes Exposition," *Timeline* 13, no. 2, (March/April 1996): 2–5; *Official Souvenir Guide, Cleveland 1936* (n.p., n.d.), 20, 22, 30–32.
24. Vacha, "Biggest Bash," 5–10; *Official Souvenir Guide*, 12–19, 21, 23–30, 38–40; Rydell, *World of Fairs*, 127.
25. Vacha, "Biggest Bash," 15–23.
26. Michael Mullen, "New York 1939–1940," in *Historical Dictionary of World's Fairs and Expositions, 1851–1988*, ed. John E. Findling and Kimberly D. Pelle (Westport, Conn.: Greenwood Press, 1990), 293–95.
27. Joseph F. Cusker, "The World of Tomorrow," in *Dawn of a New Day: The New York World's Fair, 1939/40*, ed. Helen Harrison (New York: New York University Press, 1980), 3–5; Eugene A. Santomasso, "The Design of Reason: Architecture and Planning of the 1939/40 New York World's Fair," in *Dawn of a New Day: The New York World's Fair, 1939/40*, ed. Helen Harrison (New York: New York University Press, 1980), 33. See also Burton Benedict's discussion of the thematic organization of world's fairs in *The Anthropology of World's Fairs* (London and Berkeley: Scolar Press, 1983), 27–41.
28. Bill McIlvaine, "Things to Come: The 1939 New York World's Fair," *American History Illustrated* 24 (Summer 1989): 44; Santomasso, "The Design of Reason," 33–35. A group of prominent New Yorkers had wanted to raise $250,000 to create a pre-Nazi German "Freedom Pavilion," featuring German art and culture produced before 1933 or by émigrés. But the idea was dropped in February 1939 when it became apparent there was not enough time to carry out the project before the fair opened ("Pre-Nazi Exhibit at Fair Abandoned," *New York Times*, 2 February 1939).
29. Mullen, "New York, 1939–1940," 296–97; McIlvaine, "Things to Come," 45–46; *Guide Book*, Futurama, New York World's Fair (New York, 1939), n.p.; the E. B. White quote is from Alfred Heller, "The Editor's Notebook," *World's Fair* 9, no. 2 (April–June 1989): 2.
30. McIlvaine, "Things to Come," 44; *Going to the Fair* (New York: New York World's Fair, 1939), 12–13.
31. McIlvaine, "Things to Come," 47; Mullen, "New York, 1939–1940," 248.

147

32. Rydell, *World of Fairs*, 183–87; "Programs of the Current Week," *New York Times*, 21 July 1940.

33. McIlvaine, "Things to Come," 47.

34. E. L. Doctorow, *World's Fair* (New York: Vintage, 1985); David Gelernter, *1939: The Lost World of the Fair* (New York: Free Press, 1996); John Corry, "Remembering the '39 World's Fair," *New York Times*, 22 November 1984.

35. Donald G. Larson, "San Francisco 1939–1940," in *Historical Dictionary of World's Fairs and Expositions, 1851–1988*, ed. John E. Findling and Kimberly D. Pelle (Westport, Conn.: Greenwood Press, 1990), 301; *Official Guide Book* (San Francisco: Golden Gate International Exposition, 1939), 106, 112.

36. *Official Guide Book*, 110, 113; Larson, "San Francisco 1939–1940," 301–2.

37. Larson, "San Francisco 1939–1940," 302–3; *Official Guide Book*, 45, 48, 62–63; Gertrude Atherton, *My San Francisco: A Wayward Biography* (Indianapolis, Ind., and New York: Bobbs-Merrill, 1946), 268–70; Rydell, *World of Fairs*, 85–91.

38. Larson, "San Francisco 1939–1940," 303; Rydell, *World of Fairs*, 137.

4. FAIRS IN THE ATOMIC AGE

1. Murray Morgan, *Century 21: The Story of the Seattle World's Fair, 1962* (Seattle: Acme Press, 1963), 36–60; John M. Findlay, *Magic Lands: Western Cityscapes and American Culture after 1940* (Berkeley, Calif.: University of California Press, 1992), 218–28.

2. Morgan, *Century 21*, 64–69.

3. Ibid., 81–89, 113–22; Findlay, *Magic Lands*, 215–16.

4. Paul Ashdown, "Seattle 1962," in *Historical Dictionary of World's Fairs and Expositions, 1851–1988*, ed. John E. Findling and Kimberly D. Pelle (Westport, Conn.: Greenwood Press, 1990), 319–21. The BIE was organized to regulate the number of international expositions held annually. It was a response to the multitude of expositions held in the years before World War I. The French government hosted an international meeting that approved a diplomatic convention in 1928. The BIE served as the administrative body for the convention, under the authority of the League of Nations, and was headquartered in Paris. Because the United States never ratified the League of Nations, it never felt obliged to pay much attention to BIE guidelines. Indeed, the United States only joined the convention in 1968. See Ted Allan, "The Bureau of International Expositions," in *Historical Dictionary of World's Fairs and Expositions, 1851–1988*, ed. John E. Findling and Kimberly D. Pelle (Westport, Conn.: Greenwood Press, 1990), 372–74.

5. Ogden Tanner, "Seattle Fair," *Architectural Forum* 116 (June 1962): 97–100; Russell Lynes, "Seattle Will Never Be the Same . . . ," *Harper's Magazine* 225 (July 1962): 20–21; James T. Burns Jr., "The Architecture of Century 21," *Progressive Architecture* 45, no. 6 (June 1962): 49; Findlay, *Magic Lands*, 239–45.

6. Lynes, "Seattle . . . ," 21–22; Burns, "The Architecture of Century 21," 53–54.

7. *Official Guide Book* (Seattle, Wash.: Seattle World's Fair, 1962), 8–24, 65; James Gilbert, *Redeeming Culture: American Religion in an Age of Science* (Chicago: University of Chicago Press, 1997), 308–19.

8. *Official Guide Book*, 111–16; Lynes, "Seattle . . . ," 23.

9. Ashdown, "Seattle 1962," 321; Lynes, "Seattle . . . ," 20.

10. Findlay, *Magic Lands*, 256–65; Russell Lynes, "Aftermath in Seattle," *Harper's Magazine* 232 (February 1966): 22–28.

11. Daniel T. Lawrence, "New York 1964–1965," in *Historical Dictionary of World's Fairs and Expositions, 1851–1988*, ed. John E. Findling and Kimberly D. Pelle (Westport, Conn.: Greenwood Press, 1990), 322.

12. Robert Alden and Bernard Weinraub, "World's Fair Ends Today," *New York Times*, 17 October 1965; Lawrence, "New York 1964–1965," 322–23.

13. Lawrence, "New York 1964–1965," 323–24; Vincent J. Scully Jr., "If This Is Good Architecture, God Help Us," *Life* 57, no. 9 (31 July 1964): 9.

14. *Official Guide* (New York: New York World's Fair, 1964), 204, 214–15, 220–21; Lawrence, "New York 1964–1965," 324; Scully, "If This Is Good Architecture," 9. See the special section of the *New York Times*, 19 April 1964, for a very thorough description of the fair and its attractions.

15. *Official Guide*, 53, 151–52, 170, 190.

16. *Official Guide*, 138, 147–48, 266–68. In *The Anthropology of World's Fairs* (London and Berkeley: Scolar Press, 1983), Burton Benedict counts thirty-seven commercial pavilions at the New York fair, more than at any other major fair, although the 1939–40 New York fair was close with thirty-four commercial pavilions. See his discussion of the evolution of those buildings on 24–26.

17. Lawrence, "New York 1964–1965," 326; Philip H. Dougherty, "A Stripper Lasts 2 Shows at Fair," *New York Times*, 8 May 1965.

18. Homer Bigart, "Fair Opens . . . 300 Arrested in Demonstrations," *New York Times*, 23 April 1964.

19. Robert Alden, "Fair Unable to Repay City or Finance Queens Parks," *New York Times*, 27 January 1965; Lawrence, "New York 1964–1965," 327.

20. Edith Evans Asbury, "Fair Wooing Straphanger," *New York Times*, 11 January 1965; Alden, "Fair Unable to Repay City"; Robert Alden, "World's Fair Had Deficit of $17,540,100 in 1964," *New York Times*, 6 February 1965; Robert Alden, "Committee Set Up to Publicize Fair," *New York Times*, 11 February 1965; Richard Phalon, "The World's Fair: A Fiscal Scrutiny," *New York Times*, 13 February 1965. See also the "All New for 1965" *Official Guide* for the fair, which describes the new or changed exhibits.

21. Alden and Weinraub, "World's Fair Ends Today."

22. Lawrence, "New York 1964–1965," 327–28; Alden and Weinraub, "World's Fair Ends Today."

23. Ed Christopherson, "Alaska's Centennial Show," *New York Times*, 13 November 1966; "Still Waters Lie on the Stricken Alaskan City," *Life* 63, no. 13 (1 September 1967): 24–25; Scrapbook, Alaska '67 (in the private collection of John E. Findling).

24. Shirley Eoff, "San Antonio's World's Fair/Urban Renewal Project" (unpublished paper presented at the annual meeting of the National Conference on Public History, San Diego, Calif., March 1990); James L. Mackay, "Hemisfair '68 and Paseo del Rio '38," *AIA Journal* 69 (April 1968): 48–58; Roger Montgomery, "Hemisfair '68: Prologue to Renewal," *Architectural Forum* 129 (October 1968): 84–89.

149

25. United States Pavilion, *Confluence U.S.A.* (Austin, Tex.: U.S. Pavilion, Hemis-Fair '68, E. & I. Print Co., 1968); Arbon Jack Lowe, "Hemisfair," *Americas* 20 (May 1968): 5–14.

26. Eoff, "San Antonio's World's Fair."

27. William Stimson, *A View of the Falls: An Illustrated History of Spokane* (Northridge, Calif: Windsor Publications, 1985), 85–90.

28. Stimson, *A View of the Falls*, 90–91; J. William T. Youngs, *The Fair and the Falls: Spokane's Expo '74: Transforming an American Environment* (Cheney, Wash.; Eastern Washington University Press, 1996), 295–324.

29. Dorothy R. Powers, "President Praises Spokane, Expo '74: Sees City Opening New Era," *Spokane Spokesman-Review*, 5 May 1974. See also R. W. Apple Jr., "Nixon Opens World's Fair in Spokane," *New York Times*, 5 May 1974. The complete text of Nixon's speech appears in the special exposition edition of the *Spokane Spokesman-Review*, 5 May 1974. Dave Holstrom, quoted in Larry Young, "Opening Day Goes Like Clockwork," *Spokane Spokesman-Review*, 5 May 1974.

30. *Spokane Spokesman-Review*, special exposition edition, 5 May 1974; Youngs, *The Fair and the Falls*, 367–98, 423–24; Stimson, *A View of the Falls*, 91–94. As evidence that the cold war was still a fact of international life, the *New York Times* noted the noise produced by B-52s flying in and out of nearby Fairchild Air Force Base and quoted a member of the Soviet delegation: "It is a great irony. An environment fair here and the thing that destroyed the environment in Vietnam up there" (James Sterba, "Balloons and Birds Open Expo," *New York Times*, 5 May 1974).

31. Youngs, *The Fair and the Falls*, 503–22. In 1994 a new bridge over the Spokane River was dedicated and named for King Cole.

32. *The Philadelphia Plan* (Philadelphia: Philadelphia 1976 Bicentennial Corporation, 1968), passim; "A bicentennial bumps into Mayor Rizzo," *Business Week* (22 January 1972): 22–23; Donald Janson, "Vote By '76 Panel Imperils a U.S. Expo," *New York Times*, 17 May 1972.

33. Joe Dodd, *World Class Politics: Knoxville's 1982 World's Fair, Redevelopment, and the Political Process* (Salem, Wis.: Sheffield Publishing Co., 1988), 3–5; Dick Kaukas, "The Fair: Dream or Reality," *Louisville Times*, 13 March 1982.

34. Robert Doak, "Knoxville 1982," in *Historical Dictionary of World's Fairs and Expositions, 1851–1988*, ed. John E. Findling and Kimberly D. Pelle (Westport, Conn.: Greenwood Press, 1990), 352–55; Dodd, *World Class Politics*, 14–15. See also the *Official Guide Book, The 1982 World's Fair* (Knoxville, Tenn.: Exposition Publishers, 1982), 74–89, for a list of the official sponsors.

35. The Knoxville fair was covered extensively by the *New York Times* as was the story of Butcher's financial difficulties.

36. Clive Hardy, "New Orleans 1984," in *Historical Dictionary of World's Fairs and Expositions, 1851–1988*, ed. John E. Findling and Kimberly D. Pelle (Westport, Conn.: Greenwood Press, 1990), 356–57; *The Official Guidebook*, 1984 World's Fair, New Orleans (New Orleans: Picayune Publishers, 1984), passim.

37. Hardy, "New Orleans 1984," 357–58; Frances Frank Marus, "New Orleans Blacks Plan Museum after Fair," *New York Times*, 27 April 1984; *The Official Guidebook*, 61, 68.

38. President Reagan's political advisers determined that a visit to New Orleans would take an entire weekend, would generate little public interest, and therefore was not worthwhile. Secretary of Commerce Malcolm Baldridge represented the administration at the opening ceremonies. William E. Schmidt, "New Orleans Fair Gets a Boat-Lifting, Speechifying Start," *New York Times,* 13 May 1984.

39. "Governor Expects Dismissal of 2 World's Fair Executives," *New York Times,* 3 October 1984.

40. Hardy, "New Orleans 1984," 358; see also "Former World's Fair Official Charged with Kickback Plot," *New York Times,* 6 October 1984; Wayne King, "Failed Fair Gives New Orleans a Painful Hangover," *New York Times,* 12 November 1984; "New Orleans Fair Lost $121 Million," *New York Times,* 9 Decemer 1984; "Auction Held in New Orleans to Recoup Some Fair Losses," *New York Times,* 4 January 1985; Michael Hirsley, "Fair-Sized Hangover for New Orleans," *Chicago Tribune,* 9 May 1985.

41. John McCarron, "World of Lessons from Failed Fair," *Chicago Tribune,* 3 May 1992.

42. John E. Findling, *Chicago's Great World's Fairs* (Manchester, England: Manchester University Press, 1994), 151–52; John McCarron and Daniel Egler, "Seeds of Fair's Demise Were Planted Early," *Chicago Tribune,* 23 June 1985.

43. Findling, *Chicago's Great World's Fairs,* 152; John McCarron and Daniel Egler, "Chicago's 1992 Fair Laid to Rest in 1985," *Chicago Tribune,* 21 June 1985. E. R. Shipp, "Chicago's Doubts May Dig Grave for World-Class Fairs," *New York Times,* 30 June 1985. See also Robert McClory, *The Fall of the Fair: Communities Struggle for Fairness* (Chicago: The Committee, 1986), 1–35.

44. Russell Lynes, "Goodbye to World's Fairs," *Harper's Magazine* 231 (October 1965): 28–29; Mike Royko, "Denying Politics Its Unfair Share," *Chicago Tribune,* 24 June 1985. Interestingly, in 1901 the editor of the *Canadian Magazine,* musing about the failure of the Pan-American Exposition, suggested that the era of world's fairs might be past because of the introduction of photographs in newspapers, the emergence of the ten cent magazine, and the growth of trade papers, all of which "keep the world well posted with regard to international progress" (*The Canadian Magazine* 18, no. 2 [December 1901]: 99–107).

CONCLUSION: CULTURAL DINOSAURS? WORLD'S FAIRS AND THE SURVIVAL OF THE SPECIES

1. See David Quammen's interview with paleontologist Jack Horner in *Natural Acts: A Sidelong View of Science and Nature* (New York: Schocken Books, 1985), 61–71. Horner is quoted as saying: "I don't give a shit *what* killed the dinosaurs. They dominated the earth for 140 million years. Let's stop asking why they *failed* and try to figure out why they *succeeded* so well."

2. See Mark Archbar, ed., *Manufacturing Consent: Noam Chomsky and the Media* (Montreal and Cheektowaga, N.Y.: Black Rose Books, 1994).

3. Tony Bennett, *The Birth of the Museum* (New York: Routledge, 1995), 67.

4. Penelope Harvey, *Hybrids of Modernity: Anthropology, the Nation State, and the Universal Exposition* (London: Routledge, 1996), 103.

5. *Official Descriptive and Illustrated Catalogue*, vol. 2 (London: Spicer Brothers, 1851), 1454–55.

6. Howard P. Segal, *Technological Utopianism in American Culture* (Chicago: University of Chicago Press, 1985), 125–28.

7. "Lessons of the Exposition," *Omaha Daily Bee*, 1 June 1898.

8. In addition to Segal's work just cited, see Folke T. Kihlstedt, "Utopia Realized: The World's Fairs of the 1930s," in *Imagining Tomorrow: History, Technology, and the American Future*, ed. Joseph J. Corn (Cambridge, Mass.: MIT Press, 1986), 97–118.

9. *Official Guide: Book of the Fair 1933*, quoted in Robert W. Rydell, *World of Fairs: The Century-of-Progress Expositions* (Chicago: University of Chicago Press, 1993), 98–99.

10. Scholarship on E-42 is sparse. See "Rome 1942," in *Historical Dictionary of World's Fairs and Expositions, 1851–1988*, ed. John E. Findling and Kimberly D. Pelle (Westport, Conn.: Greenwood Press, 1990), 405–6, for a start.

11. Rosalind H. Williams, *Dream Worlds: Mass Consumption in Late Nineteenth-Century France* (Berkeley, Calif.: University of California Press, 1982).

12. Roland Marchand, "Corporate Imagery and Popular Education: World's Fairs and Expositions in the United States, 1893–1940," in *Consumption and American Culture*, ed. David E. Nye and Carl Pedersen (Amsterdam: VU University Press, 1991), 18–33.

13. The secretary of commerce was Luther H. Hodges, and his quote appears in John M. Findlay, *Magic Lands: Western Cityscapes and American Culture after 1940* (Berkeley, Calif.: University of California Press, 1992), 238. For information on the Seattle fair, see James Gilbert, *Redeeming Culture: American Religion in an Age of Science* (Chicago: University of Chicago Press, 1997), 297–319. For information on the 1958 Brussels Universal Exposition, consult Rydell, *World of Fairs*, 193–211; and Brigitte Schroeder-Gudehus and David Cloutier, "Popularizing Science and Technology during the Cold War: Brussels 1958," in *Fair Representations: World's Fairs and the Modern World*, ed. Robert W. Rydell and Nancy E. Gwinn (Amsterdam: VU University Press, 1994), 157–80.

14. Schroeder-Gudehus and Cloutier, "Popularizing Science and Technology," 179.

15. *The Hannover Principles: Design for Sustainability* (New York: W. McDonough Architects, 1992), 20. This work was reissued in 1998. Subsequent references are to the 1992 edition.

16. Ibid., 20,

17. Ibid., 58.

18. See especially 291–307 in Umberto Eco, *Travels in Hyperreality* (San Diego: Harcourt Brace Jovanovich, 1986).

19. *The Hannover Principles*, 59.

SUGGESTIONS FOR FURTHER READING

GENERAL WORKS

Before 1977 world's fair scholarship was seldom seen. Only a very few publications had a wide audience; most writing about fairs and expositions was relegated to state and city historical society journals and isolated references in larger works on cultural, technological, or architectural history. In 1977, however, John Allwood published *The Great Exhibitions* (London: Cassell and Collier Macmillan), a heavily illustrated, comprehensive history of fairs and expositions that remains one of the best general treatments of the subject. Allwood's book inspired a heightened awareness of fairs and the role they have played in the cultural evolution of the world, and it encouraged other scholars to consider fairs as an appropriate subject for research. A number of books on fairs appeared in the late 1970s and 1980s, many of which dealt with a specific fair. Some of those books, however, adopted a thematic approach and dealt with several fairs, such as Robert W. Rydell, *All the World's a Fair: Visions of Empire at American International Expositions, 1876–1916* (Chicago: University of Chicago Press, 1984), which analyzes the institutionalization of racist thought in America between 1876 and 1916 through its representation at major American fairs. Burton Benedict, ed., *The Anthropology of World's Fairs* (London and Berkeley: Scolar Press, 1983), focuses principally on the 1915 Panama-Pacific International Exposition but also looks generally at fairs as social ritual. Another way to analyze fairs is through their contribution to nationalism and imperialism, which Paul Greenhalgh does in *Ephemeral Vistas: The Expositions Universelles, Great Exhibitions and World's Fairs, 1851–1939* (Manchester, England: Manchester University Press, 1988).

In 1992 Robert W. Rydell provided a general history of fairs in his long introduction to *The Books of the Fairs: Materials about World's Fairs, 1834–1916, in the Smithsonian Institution Libraries* (Chicago: American Library Association, 1992), a comprehensive listing of the world's fair resources held by the Smithsonian Institution. *The Books of the Fairs* is the best place to begin assembling a bibliography of materials related to a specific fair or fair-related theme. John E. Findling and Kimberly D. Pelle, eds., *Historical Dictionary of World's Fairs and Expositions, 1851–1988* (Westport, Conn.: Greenwood Press, 1990), remains the basic reference work on fairs and includes essays on ninety-four fairs and a good deal of bibliographic information. A recent general work of value, published in conjunction with the 1992 Seville Exposicion Universal, is Luis Calvo Teixeira, *Universal Exhibitions: The World in Seville* (Barcelona: Labor, 1992).

A number of books and articles take a more theoretical approach to world's fairs, attempting to link them with broader cultural movements or historical trends. A recent example of this genre is E. A. Herman, *The Inglorious Arts of Peace: Exhibitions in Canadian Society during the Nineteenth Century* (Toronto: University of Toronto Press, 1999). Two books, Julie K. Brown, *Contesting Images: Photography and the World's Columbian Exposition* (Tucson, Ariz.: University of Arizona Press, 1994), and Eric Breitbart, *A World on Display: Photographs from the St. Louis World's Fair 1904* (Albuquerque, N.Mex.: University of New Mexico Press, 1997), discuss the way photographs of world's fair exhibits, especially those of "living anthropology exhibits," can be read to understand what they were supposed to connote to contemporary fairgoers. In "Festivals of Nationhood: The International Exhibitions" (*Australian Cultural History*, ed. Samuel Lewis Goldberg and F. B. Smith [Cambridge: Cambridge University Press, 1988], 158–77), Graeme Davison analyzes the role of world's fairs in shaping the modern nation-state. Micaela Di Leonardo, *Exotics at Home: Anthropologies, Others, American Modernity* (Chicago: University of Chicago Press, 1998), studies the lingering impact of the White City/Midway Plaisance dichotomy on subsequent American cultural developments, while Paul Greenhalgh, "Education, Entertainment and Politics: Lessons from the Great International Exhibitions" (*The New Museology*, ed. Peter Vergo [London: Reaktion, 1989], 74–89), compares contemporary museum policies with the didactic mission of world's fairs. A look at fairs from the viewpoints of planners and visitors can be found in Robert Brain, *Going to the Fair: Readings in the Culture of Nineteenth-Century Exhibitions* (Cambridge, England: Whipple Museum of the History of Science, 1993). In *Becoming Modern in Toronto* (Toronto: University of Toronto Press, 1997), Keith Walden shows how the annual Toronto Industrial Exhibition (which later became known as the Canadian National Exhibition) brought an increasingly modern outlook to the city in the late nineteenth century. Finally, two works that look at the most recent fairs and their impact are Penelope Harvey, *Hybrids of Modernity: Anthropology, the Nation State, and the Universal Exhibition* (London: Routledge, 1996), which uses the 1992 Seville exposition as a model for an analysis of "auto-anthropology," and Carl Malamud, *A World's Fair for the Global Village* (Cambridge, Mass.: MIT Press, 1997), which reveals how the web of world's fairs served as a prototype for the modern day computer-driven World Wide Web.

A few books trace the evolution of certain types of exhibits throughout the history of world's fairs. K. G. Beauchamp, ed., *Exhibiting Electricity* (London: Institution of Electrical Engineers, 1997), and Jane Shadell Spillman, *Glass from World's Fairs, 1851–1904* (Corning, N.Y.: Corning Museum of Glass, 1986), are two good examples. For a comprehensive discussion of world's fair architecture over the years, see Wolfgang Friebe, *Architektur der Weltausstellungen: 1850 bis 1970* (Stuttgart: Kohlhammer, 1983). This book is also available in an English-language edition: *Buildings of the World Exhibitions* (Leipzig: Edition Leipiz, 1985).

FAIRS IN THE AGE OF INDUSTRIALISM'S ADVANCE

For most of the specific fairs discussed in this book, good sources of additional information are the official guidebooks for the fairs and contemporary newspaper accounts. The guidebooks provide the basic information about the fairs—their exhibits, their entertainment opportunities, and their site layouts—often with plentiful illustrations. Readers should be aware, however, that guidebooks were often prepared some months before the fair actually opened, and therefore they do not reflect late changes in exhibits or attractions. Host city newspapers usually devoted large amounts of space to a world's fair, providing much detail to their readers who might wish to visit the fair. Newspapers also usually gave good coverage of the plans and preparations for the fair and did not hesitate to report on any political or economic controversy accompanying the event.

Most major fairs have attracted a significant amount of scholarly attention, particularly in the last twenty years, although the Crystal Palace Exhibition of 1851 has enjoyed a longer period of interest. Patrick Beaver, *The Crystal Palace* (London: Hugh Evelyn Ltd., 1970), is a history of the building that includes much information about the exhibition as well, and Eric de Maré, *London 1851: The Year of the Great Exhibition* (London: Folio Society, 1972), contains descriptive accounts that help place the exhibition into its historical context. Perhaps the most comprehensive history of the Crystal Palace Exhibition is C. H. Gibbs-Smith, *The Great Exhibition of 1851* (London: Victoria and Albert Museum, 1950), which is replete with period photographs and other excellent illustrations.

For recent analyses of the New York Crystal Palace Exhibition of 1853–54, readers must consult scholarly articles. Ivan D. Steen discusses the importance of the exhibition to New York City in "America's First World's Fair: The Exhibition of the Industry of All Nations at New York's Crystal Palace, 1853–1854" (*New York Historical Society Quarterly,* 47 [July 1963]: 257–87), while Charles Hirschfeld, in "America on Exhibition: The New York Crystal Palace" (*American Quarterly* 9 [Summer 1957]: 101–16), provides a thorough description of the exposition and the contemporary reaction to it.

The Philadelphia Centennial International Exhibition of 1876 has been relatively well served by historians. An older descriptive work, with an excellent bibliography of contemporary writing about the exhibition, is John Maass, *The Glorious Enterprise: The Centennial Exhibition of 1876 and H. J. Schwartzmann, Architect-in-Chief* (Watkins Glen, N.Y.: Institute for the Study of Universal History Through Arts/American Life Foundation, 1973). In 1976 many of the exhibits from the Centennial Exhibition were displayed in the Smithsonian Institution's Arts and Industries Museum on the Mall in Washington, D.C.; a very useful book published in conjunction with that exhibit is Robert C. Post, ed., *1876: A Centennial Exhibition* (Washington, D.C.: National Museum of History and Technology, Smithsonian Institution, 1976). The activities of the suffrage movement's leaders at the Centennial Exhibition are recounted in Matilda Joslyn Gage, *The Declaration of the Rights of Women: 1876* (Aberdeen, S.Dak.: North Plains Press, 1975). A good example of the many contemporary accounts is James L. Dale, *What Ben Beverly Saw at the Great Exposition, by a Chicago Lawyer* (Chicago: Centennial Publishing Co., 1876), which describes the sights in Fairmount Park through the eyes of a fictitious visitor. In addition there are a number of excellent contemporary picture books on this fair; among the best are James D. McCabe, *The Illustrated History of the Centennial Exhibition* (Philadelphia: National Publishing Co., 1876), and Thompson Westcott, *Centennial Portfolio* (Philadelphia: Thomas Hunter, 1876). Finally Russell Lynes notes the great impact of the Centennial Exhibition (and other expositions) on American public tastes in *The Tastemakers* (New York: Harper, 1954).

For information about the anthropological exhibits at the southern fairs of the late nineteenth and early twentieth centuries, see Robert W. Rydell, *All the World's a Fair.* For a discussion of the economic motivations of the planners of those fairs, see John E. Findling, "Opening the Door to the World: International Expositions in the South, 1881–1907" (*Studies in American Culture,* ed. Dennis Hall, 19, no. 2 [1996]: 29–38). Also important are several recent Ph.D. dissertations: Bruce G. Harvey, "World's Fairs in a Southern Accent: Atlanta, Nashville, Charleston, 1895–1902" (Vanderbilt University, 1998) and Judy L. Larson, "Three Southern World's Fairs: Cotton States and International Exposition, Atlanta, 1895; Tennessee Centennial, Nashville, 1897; South Carolina Inter-State and West Indian Exposition, Charleston, 1901–02: Creating Regional Self-Portraits through Expositions" (Emory University, 1998).

Among all American expositions, the 1893 World's Columbian Exposition in Chicago has generated the most scholarly interest. Contemporary descriptive and pictorial accounts abound, and well-known authors of the day—including Henry Adams, Hubert Howe Bancroft, and William Dean Howells—wrote about the fair. More recent studies include a fine general treatment by R. Reid Badger, *The Great American Fair: The World's Columbian Exposition and American Culture* (Chicago: N. Hall, 1979). Robert Muccigrosso, *Celebrating the New World: Chicago's Columbian Exposition of 1893* (Chicago: I. R. Dee, 1993), is a very accessible recent account. James B. Gilbert, *Perfect Cities: Chicago's Utopias of 1893* (Chicago: University of Chicago Press, 1991), includes a study of the exposition as a "perfect city," while Neil Harris, *Cultural Excursions: Marketing Appetites and Cultural Tastes in Modern America* (Chicago: University of Chicago Press, 1990), includes a lengthy discussion of the place of fairs in American culture, with a focus on the World's Columbian Exposition. Jean Madeline Weimann, *The Fair Women* (Chicago: Academy Chicago, 1981), is a lengthy and detailed treatment of the women's building and women's activities at the exposition, and Julie K. Brown, *Contesting Images: Photography and the World's Columbian Exposition* (Tucson, Ariz.: University of Arizona Press, 1994), is very comprehensive on the importance of both professional and amateur photography at the fair.

The centennial of the World's Columbian Exposition produced other works of interest on the fair, most notably Neil Harris et al., eds., *Grand Illusions: Chicago's World's Fair of 1893* (Chicago: Chicago Historical Society, 1993), a book published to accompany a major exhibit at the Chicago Historical Society, and Peter B. Hales, *Constructing the Fair: Platinum Photographs by C. D. Arnold of the World's Columbian Exposition* (Chicago: Art Institute of Chicago, 1993). See also Norman Bolotin and Christine Laing, *The World's Columbian Exposition* (Washington, D.C.: Preservation Press, 1992), a publication of the National Trust for Historic Preservation that emphasizes the buildings and exhibits.

The 1894 California Midwinter International Exposition, coming as it did in the wake of the World's Columbian Exposition, has not been much studied, but Raymond H. Clary, *The Making of Golden Gate Park: The Early Years: 1865–1906* (San Francisco: Don't Call It Frisco Press, 1987), devotes a long chapter to it.

FAIRS OF THE IMPERIAL ERA

The Trans-Mississippi and International Exposition in Omaha has attracted relatively little attention from scholars, although Robert W. Rydell devotes a chapter to it in *All the World's a Fair*. Readers may also consult Kenneth Alfers, "Triumph of the West: The Trans-Mississippi Exposition" (*Nebraska History* 53, no. 3 [Fall 1972]: 313–29), and William Kahrl, "Omaha Unites a Nation" (*World's Fair* 3, no. 3 [Summer 1983]: 1–5).

For the 1901 Pan-American Exposition in Buffalo, see the relevant chapter in William Irwin, *The New Niagara: Tourism, Technology, and the Landscape of Niagara Falls, 1776–1917* (University Park, Penn.: Pennsylvania State University Press, 1996), which places the fair into the context of the development of Buffalo and nearby Niagara Falls. Biographies of McKinley detail the president's visit to and assassination at the fair; see, for example, Lewis L. Gould, *The Presidency of William McKinley* (Lawrence, Kans.: Regents Press of Kansas, 1980). Contemporary magazines published extensively about the fair. Particularly useful in that regard are the August 1901 issue of *World's Work* and the September 1901 issue of *The Cosmopolitan*. Richard H. Barry, *Snap Shots on the Midway of the Pan-Am Expo* (Buffalo, N.Y.: R. A. Reid, 1901), presents a great deal of information and numerous pictures of the many midway attractions.

The large, extravagant 1904 Louisiana Purchase International Exposition in St. Louis has not attracted the number of scholars that the World's Columbian Exposition has, but the approaching centennial of the fair may change that situation. Contemporary periodicals such as *Scribner's Magazine* and *Architectural Record* provided detailed accounts of the fair for prospective visitors. A concerted effort by the Missouri Historical Society to commemorate the fair and to record the reminiscences of fair visitors as its seventy-fifth anniversary approached resulted in Martha R. Clevenger, ed., *Indescribably Grand: Diaries and Letters from the 1904 World's Fair* (St. Louis, Mo.: Missouri Historical Society Press, 1996), and Dorothy Daniels Birk, *The World Came to St. Louis* (St. Louis: Bethany Press, 1979). *Gateway Heritage*, the journal of the Missouri Historical Society, has published a number of articles on the exposition in recent years. See, for example, Karen M. Keefer, "Dirty Water and Clean Toilets: Medical Aspects of the 1904 Louisiana Purchase Exposition" (*Gateway Heritage* 9, no. 1 [Summer 1988]: 33–37), which treats the medical problems associated with the large fair and many visitors.

The basic book on Portland's Lewis and Clark Centennial and American Pacific Exposition and Oriental Fair of 1905 is Carl Abbott, *The Great Extravaganza: Portland and the Lewis and Clark Exposition* (Portland: Oregon Historical Society, 1981), which is richly illustrated. Abbott also discusses the influence of the fair on Portland's urban development in *Portland: Planning, Politics, and Growth in a Twentieth Century City* (Lincoln, Nebr.: University of Nebraska Press, 1983).

A good modern survey of the 1909 Alaska-Yukon-Pacific Exposition in Seattle is

George Frykman, "The Alaska-Yukon-Pacific International Exposition" (*Pacific Northwest Quarterly*, 53, no. 3 [July 1962]: 89–99). See also Robert W. Rydell, "Visions of Empire" (*Pacific Historical Review* 52, no. 1 [February 1983]: 37–65), which discusses both the Portland and Seattle expositions in relation to their efforts to expand American commerce across the Pacific.

Burton Benedict, ed., *The Anthropology of World's Fairs*, mentioned earlier, remains the standard work on San Francisco's Panama-Pacific International Exposition in 1915. In his recent book, *World's Fairs and the End of Progress* (Corte Madera, Calif.: World's Fair, Inc., 1999), Alfred Heller discusses certain aspects of the exposition. This fair produced several worthwhile contemporary accounts, particularly of its art and architecture. Among those are Juliet James, *Palaces and Courts of the Exposition* (San Francisco: California Book Company, 1915); Eugen Neuhaus, *The Art of the Exposition* (San Francisco: P. Elder and Company, 1915), and Edward H. Hurlbut, "Features of the Panama-Pacific Exposition" (*Overland*, no. 66 [November 1915]: 379–88).

For the 1915–16 Panama California Exposition in San Diego, the best modern source is probably Richard F. Pourade, *Gold in the Sun* (San Diego: Union-Tribune Pub. Co., 1965), volume five of a multivolume history of the city. Also useful is Gregory Montes, "Balboa Park: 1909–1911: The Rise and Fall of the Olmsted Plan" (*Journal of San Diego History* 28 [Winter 1982]: 46–57), which details some of the politics involved in the fair's origins and planning. Finally, Florence Christman, *The Romance of Balboa Park* (San Diego: San Diego Historical Society, 1985), contains good descriptions of the exposition's buildings, many of which still stand in the park.

FAIRS BETWEEN THE WORLD WARS

Readers wishing to know more about the influential 1924–25 British Empire Exhibition at Wembley and the 1925 Exposition Internationale des Arts Décoratifs et Industriels Modernes in Paris should start with John Allwood, *The Great Exhibitions* (London: Cassell and Collier Macmillan, 1977). The Wembley exhibition is also discussed in John M. McKenzie, *Propaganda and Empire* (Manchester, England: Manchester University Press, 1984), and Paul Greenhalgh, *Ephemeral Vistas: The Expositions Universelles, Great Exhibitions and World's Fairs, 1851–1939* (Manchester, England: Manchester University Press, 1988), while virtually every history of the art deco movement touches on the Paris exposition.

Little recent work has been done on the overlooked Philadelphia Sesqui-Centennial Exposition of 1926. Its High Street colonial reconstruction receives mention in Alan Axelrod, ed., *The Colonial Revival in America* (New York: W. W. Norton, 1985), and Robert W. Rydell, *World of Fairs: The Century-of-Progress Expositions* (Chicago: University of Chicago Press, 1993), discusses its racial aspects. Also, see in particular chapter 7 of Steven Conn, *Museums and American Intellectual Life, 1876–1926* (Chicago: University of Chicago Press, 1998.) Even less has been done with the 1928 Pacific Southwest Exposition in Long Beach, and researchers will have to rely on contemporary newspaper and magazine sources, several of which were reprinted in John W. Ryckman, ed., *Story of an Epochal Event in California: The Pacific Southwest Exposition* (Long Beach: Long Beach Chamber of Commerce, 1929).

The architecture and exhibits of Chicago's Century of Progress Exposition of 1933–34 are the focus of John E. Findling, *Chicago's Great World's Fairs* (Manchester, England: Manchester University Press, 1994). Robert W. Rydell, in *World of Fairs*, emphasizes the role of science and the treatment of African Americans at the fair. Cathy Cahan and Richard Cahan, "The Lost City of the Depression" (*Chicago History* 4 [Winter 1976–77]: 233–42), present a retrospective of the fair through the recollections of a key official, and Susan Talbot-Stanaway, "The Giant Jewel" (*Chicago History* 22, no. 2 [July 1993]: 4–23), discusses the architecture of the fair, with an emphasis on the use of bright colors. Lenox Lohr, the fair's general manager, wrote an excellent account of his perspective of the fair in *Fair Management: The Story of the Century of Progress* (Chicago: Cuneo Press, 1952).

For San Diego's second world's fair, the 1935–36 California Pacific International Exposition, consult Richard F. Pourade, *The Rising Tide* (San Diego: Union-Tribune Pub. Co., 1968), volume six of Pourade's history of the city, and Florence Christman, *The Romance of Balboa Park*. A popular magazine account of the fair is Sam Ervine, "The 1935 Exposition" (*San Diego Magazine* [June 1965]: 65–71, 95).

There are a number of works on the 1939–40 New York World's Fair, some of which were prompted by the golden anniversary of the event. One of the most useful is Helen Harrison, ed., *Dawn of a New Day: The New York World's Fair, 1939/40* (New York: New York University Press, 1980), a book designed to accompany a major exhibit on the fair curated by Harrison at the Queens Museum in Flushing, New York. Though heavily pictorial, it contains several informative essays on different aspects of the fair. See also Larry Zim, Mel Lerner, and Herbert Rolfes, *The World of Tomorrow: The 1939 New York World's Fair* (New York: Harper and Row, 1988), and Barbara Cohen, Steven Heller, and Seymour Chwast, *Trylon and Perisphere* (New York: Abrams, 1989), both of which contain excellent photographs. David Gelernter, *1939: The Lost World of the Fair* (New York: Free Press, 1995), weaves interesting descriptions of the fair into a fictional love story. Joseph J. Corn and Brian Horrigan, *Yesterday's Tomorrows: Past Visions of the American Future* (Washington, D.C., and New York: Smithsonian Institution Traveling Exhibition Service and Summit Books, 1984), discuss the fair's efforts to define a future America. Finally, Grover Whalen, *Mr. New York* (New York: Putnam, 1955), is an autobiography of one of the principal fair managers.

San Francisco's 1939–40 fair, the Golden Gate International Exposition, is the subject of Richard Reinhardt, *Treasure Island: San Francisco's Exposition Years* (San Francisco: Scrimshaw Press, 1973). Reinhardt also discusses the fair in "The Other Fair" (*American Heritage* 40, no. 4 [May/June 1989]: 42–53), on the occasion of its fiftieth anniversary. For the architecture of the fair, see "San Francisco Golden Gate Exposition 1939" (*Architectural Forum* 70 [June 1939]: 463–500).

FAIRS OF THE ATOMIC AGE

For information on the 1958 Brussels Universal Exposition and the controversial U.S. Pavilion there that influenced the Century 21 Exposition in Seattle four years later, consult Robert H. Haddow, *Pavilions of Plenty: Exhibiting American Culture Abroad in the 1950s* (Washington, D.C.: Smithsonian Institution Press, 1997), and Robert W. Rydell, *World of Fairs* (193–211). The Seattle fair itself is well covered in

Morgan Murray, *Century 21: The Story of the Seattle World's Fair, 1962* (Seattle: Acme Press, 1963), written just after the close of the event, and John M. Findlay, *Magic Lands: Western Cityscapes and American Culture after 1940* (Berkeley, Calif.: University of California Press, 1992), which puts Century 21 into a broad regional context. James Gilbert, *Redeeming Culture: American Religion in an Age of Science* (Chicago: University of Chicago Press, 1997), draws connections between scientific and religious pavilions at the Seattle exposition.

The New York World's Fair of 1964–65 is best studied through contemporary magazine and newspaper articles, although Robert Caro's biography of Robert Moses, *The Power Broker: Robert Moses and the Fall of New York* (New York: Knopf, 1974), devotes considerable space to Moses's involvement with the fair and his responsibility for its financial failure. A souvenir book of the fair, *New York World's Fair 1964/1965: Official Souvenir Book* (New York: Time-Life, 1964), contains an array of pictures and textual information about the event.

Two articles that place San Antonio's HemisFair '68 into an urban renewal context are James L. MacKay, "HemisFair '68 and Paseo del Rio" (*American Institute of Architects Journal* 69 [April 1968]: 48–58), and Roger Montgomery, "HemisFair '68: Prologue to Renewal" (*Architectural Forum* 129 [October 1968]: 84–89). The effort to connect the fair with Latin America is described in Arbon Jack Love, "Hemis-Fair" (*Americas* [May 1968]: 5–14).

Two books succeed in presenting the history of Spokane's Expo '74. William Stimson, *A View of the Falls: An Illustrated History of Spokane* (Northridge, Calif.: Windsor Publications, 1985), places the fair into the larger history of the city, while J. William T. Youngs, *The Fair and the Falls: Spokane's Expo '74: Transforming an American Environment* (Cheney, Wash.: Eastern Washington University Press, 1996), emphasizes the fair itself and the changes it brought to Spokane.

Very little scholarly work has yet been done on the Knoxville fair of 1982 or the New Orleans fair of 1984 at least partly because the records for those events have not yet been completely opened to scholars due to ongoing litigation. Joe Dodd, *World Class Politics: Knoxville's 1982 World's Fair, Redevelopment, and the Political Process* (Cheney, Wis.: Sheffield Publishing Co., 1988), presents the fair from the viewpoint of one of its principal opponents. A more positive side of the fair is seen in Terry McWilliams, "City on the River Showed the World a Thing or Two" (*World's Fair* 3, no. 1 [Winter 1983]: 5–8). For the New Orleans fair, Joshua Mann Pailet, *The World's Fair, New Orleans* (New Orleans: Gallery for Fine Photography, 1987), is an uncritical book of fine photography. The political story of the never-held Chicago fair of 1992 is recounted by an opponent of the fair in Robert McClory, *The Fall of the Fair: Communities Struggle for Fairness* (Chicago: The Committee, 1986). John E. Findling, *Chicago's Great World's Fairs*, also devotes space to the effort to stage a fair in Chicago.

VIDEO RESOURCES

Since the mid-1980s videographers have produced videotapes of many of America's world's fairs. For the older fairs those videos are based on still pictures and, occasionally, interviews with persons who visited the fair or historians who have studied the event, while for the more recent fairs, the videos incorporate 8mm or 16mm film or videotapes used in television programming, as well as interviews with planners, managers, and visitors.

Among exposition videos, two deal with fairs generally. "Come to the Fairs" (video, 58 min., PBS, Washington, D.C., 1988), episode 6 in the public television production of *A Walk through the Twentieth Century with Bill Moyers*, focuses on the major twentieth century fairs up to and including the 1982 Knoxville exposition. In 1998 the History Channel's series *Modern Marvels* released "World's Fairs: Visions of the Future" (50 min., Hearst Entertainment and Actuality Productions, New York City), which deals with the 1851 Crystal Palace Exhibition, the 1893 World's Columbian Exposition, the 1933–34 Century of Progress Exposition, and the two New York World's Fairs of 1939–40 and 1964–65.

For specific fairs the following videos are available: the 1894 California Midwinter International Exposition, *The Fantastic Fair* (29 min., the Order of Fine Fellows, San Francisco, 1983); the 1898 Trans-Mississippi and International Exposition, *Westward the Empire: Omaha's World's Fair of 1898* (57 min., UNO Television, Omaha, Neb., 1998); the 1904 Louisiana Purchase International Exposition, *A World on Display* (53 min., by Eric Breitbart, New Deal Films, Corrales, N.Mex., 1994); the 1915 Panama-Pacific International Exposition, *1915: Panama Pacific Fair* (28 min., by Burton Benedict, Lowie Museum of Anthropology, Berkeley, Calif., 1984); the 1933 Century of Progress Exposition, *Ford and a Century of Progress* (15 min., New Deal Films as part of *World's Fair Archival Video*, vol. 1, which also contains *Scenes from the New York World's Fair for 1940*, Corrales, N.Mex., 1991). In 1987 the Towne Ford Museum produced *Ford at the 1934–35 Fairs* (48 min., Towne Ford Museum, Sacramento, Calif.) covering the 1934 season at the Century of Progress Exposition and the 1935 season at the California Pacific International Exposition.

The 1939 New York World's Fair can be seen in *The World of Tomorrow*, originally a television production, but now available in several video versions. Most accessible is a 33-minute video produced by Direct Cinemas, Ltd., Santa Monica, Calif., 1992. For the 1964–65 New York World's Fair, there is *The 1964 World's Fair: Relieve* [sic] *the Wonder* (60 min., Janson Video, Harrington Park, N.J., 1996). The 1974 Spokane fair can be viewed in *Reflections on the River: EXPO '74* (60 min., KSPS Public Television, Spokane, Wash., 1994). The 1984 New Orleans fair is portrayed in two videos: *World's Fair Highlights* (29 min., WDSU TV, New Orleans, 1984) and *The Great Celebration: World's Fair '84* (30 min., WDSU TV, New Orleans, 1984).

INDEX

165